THE
YEAR
THEY
SOLD
WALL
STREET

THE
YEAR
THEY
SOLD
WALL
STREET

Tim Carrington

Houghton Mifflin Company
Boston · 1985

Library of Congress Cataloging in Publication Data

Carrington, Tim.
The year they sold Wall Street.

Includes index.
1. Shearson/American Express Inc. 2. Consolidation
and merger of corporations — United States. I. Title.
HD2746.5.C37 1985   332.6'2'097471   85-14219
ISBN 0-395-34394-1

Printed in the United States of America

P 10 9 8 7 6 5 4 3 2 1

For Merrill

They were a race
Most nervous, energetic, swift and wasteful,
And maddened by the dry and beautiful light
Although not knowing their madness.
So they built . . .

— *Stephen Vincent Benét*

The Congress must be made to recognize the threat to our
basic system posed by the specter of a handful of giant financial
conglomerates dominating the scene.

— *Robert E. Linton*
Chief Executive Officer
Drexel Burnham Lambert, Inc.

Acknowledgments

Many individuals in the financial business interrupted already strenuous schedules to discuss with me aspects of the story told in this book. My recounting of the events in these pages is based on the best recollections of the dozens of people involved, and I am enormously appreciative of their time.

There isn't space to name all of those who contributed both information and insights. In addition, many individuals wished to remain anonymous in their interviews with me, and I will respect that wish. I do want to express special thanks to Sanford Weill, James Robinson, Peter Cohen, and Salim Lewis, who provided information about the merger of Shearson Loeb Rhoades and American Express. Many other officials of those two companies were also helpful. I also extend special thanks to Harry Jacobs of Prudential Bache.

I also wish to express appreciation to the *Wall Street Journal* for setting a standard of reporting I endeavored to meet in this book and for imbuing its staff with enthusiasm for a good story wherever one is to be found.

I must also express gratitude to Nan Talese, who has deepened my appreciation for the editor's art of lending shape and coherence to sometimes unruly material. I also thank Charlotte Sheedy for her tireless support and her love for works in progress. Judith Weiss and Doreen Conrad provided word processing services, and I thank them for their precision and care.

Lastly, I am indebted to my wife for her patience and her perspective during what was a draining preoccupation for me. And I thank my son for his ability to provide laughter and welcome diversion.

1

The two men had agreed to meet at eight o'clock on August 29, 1980, within the generous portal of the Stock Exchange Luncheon Club. They had only a nodding acquaintance at the time, although the many meetings that followed this first encounter would make them intimate colleagues. They did start off with one thing in common, however: a name, which was Sandy.

For Sandy Weill, the chairman and chief executive officer of the powerful securities house Shearson Loeb Rhoades, it stood for Sanford; for Sandy Lewis, managing partner of the small and barely known S. B. Lewis & Company, it was a nickname used from birth in place of his given name, Salim.

As he walked to the Exchange from his office at 76 Beaver Street, Lewis felt grateful that Weill had agreed to the breakfast meeting, which Lewis had proposed a few days earlier over the telephone. Weill, Lewis later learned, wasn't much of a morning person and generally avoided matutinal business sessions. By contrast, Lewis often arose as early as five o'-clock, thrived during the early hours, and sometimes jangled people out of bed to talk about something on his mind.

At forty-one, Lewis was a tall, deep-chested man; his shoulders were slightly stooped; his head set forward. He had close-cropped reddish hair flecked with gray, and though he owned several pairs of glasses, he most often wore a round rimless set with thin gold earpieces. His eyes were a clear, cobalt blue.

The walk to the Exchange was no more than five minutes for him, because Wall Street — the accepted term for the area of New York extending south from Park Place — is, above all, compact. The streets seem too narrow, the buildings too tall, and the sidewalks hopelessly inadequate to contain the press of people who travel them during the business hours. The area is also filled with landmarks of America's financial history. En route to the Exchange, which functions as the nexus of the financial enclave, Lewis walked past the headquarters of Brown Brothers Harriman, the intensely private banking concern, the headquarters of J. P. Morgan, and Federal Hall Memorial, where George Washington had taken his first oath of office. There he saw a statue of the first President, turned toward the Stock Exchange building across the street, as though poised to salute the world of finance that had grown up around this early governmental structure.

The securities industry in 1980 employed some 213,400 people in the United States, of whom about 84,000 were with firms in New York City. Of those, the preponderance worked in the Wall Street area. In that year, the securities business served some 29.8 million investors. More of those lived in New York City than in any other urban area; California was the state that furnished the securities business with more customers than any other in the union. Despite its geographic scope, though, the business itself usually was identified by the street where it began — Wall Street.

Wall Street was the site of much of Lewis' personal history as well. His father, Salim Lewis, had started there in the late 1920s and become a legendary figure, running the gutsy trading firm of Bear, Stearns & Company from the 1940s until his death, in 1978. Sandy Lewis' parentage also provided an immediate link to Sandy Weill: it was Bear Stearns where in 1955 Weill had gotten his first job on Wall Street, as a runner. Sandy Weill had an indelible impression of the elder Lewis, a shrewd, bold entrepreneur, known not only for his trading skills but also for his tough manner and his salty tongue. Weill, like others, recalled being afraid of him.

Wall Street was relatively calm at eight o'clock. A few dowdy secretaries and clerks bustled about. (Wall Street workers looked older and less fashion-conscious than those in midtown.) The crush of workers would arrive around nine-thirty, in advance of the ten o'clock opening of stock trading. It was also the Friday before Labor Day, which meant that many of the financial people had already left the sweltering city for the beaches of Long Island or the bluffs of Martha's Vineyard or Nantucket to enjoy the last of the summer's long weekends. The week after Labor Day was considered the beginning of a new season for the stock market. Lewis' mission on August 29 was to introduce an idea that he hoped would usher the investment firm of Shearson Loeb Rhoades, and ultimately the financial community itself, into a new era.

The plan, which Lewis had been thinking about for some time, called for the merger of Sandy Weill's Shearson Loeb Rhoades with American Express. The idea was to establish a conglomerate dedicated to the business of money — the money people deposited and saved, the money people spent, the money people invested. But the combining of all financial services under one roof was contrary to the financial system that had prevailed since the New Deal. Much of the legislation enacted in the years following the Great Crash of 1929 was based on the concept that different financial services must be kept separate. Most significant was the Glass-Steagall Act of 1933, which mandated the separation of banks and securities firms. Also, there had long been a mistrust of giant financial institutions. In 1927, Congress passed the McFadden Act, which barred interstate branching by banks and provided competitive protection for thousands of small, independent banks throughout the United States. The laws helped foster separate cultures within the country's financial business.

In 1980, most securities firms considered themselves part of a business, and indeed a culture, that was wholly distinct from other American corporations involved in industry and commerce and from other financial companies, such as the banks or American Express. Concentrated on the southern tip of Manhattan, the people of Wall Street were proud to have a language and a set of practices and habits that were theirs alone.

At the Stock Exchange Luncheon Club, where Weill and Lewis were to meet, the past presides like a proud, somewhat tattered ancestor. The elevators open into a spacious anteroom, whose gray marble floors are molded into gentle grooves from wear. The walls feature colossal heads of moose and bison, beneath which are green-felt bulletin boards bearing lists of delinquent dues-payers. In the center of the room is a free-standing bronze statue of a bull and a bear, locked in their immortal combat. Along one wall is a long glass case containing miniatures of this piece of financial iconography, along with a sprinkling of items for sale — neckties, madras belts, and cigars.

The dining room itself is a vast, high-ceilinged room, painted a muted green, with gold leaf on the moldings and a few corners where the chipped paint reveals the white plaster beneath. By about eight-thirty the place is filled with people from every stratum of Wall Street life. There are floor brokers, who handle customer orders on the trading floor, wearing pale blue jackets and name badges. They usually cluster at long dormitory-style tables to gulp down coffee and gossip about what is happening in the stock market. Messengers, or "squads," as they are called, canter into the room with pink message slips destined for some trader or broker. Often, one of the well-tailored lords of finance glides into the clattering room for a meal. It is a place in which one can appear democratic and informal and feel a bit closer to the heart of things.

That the Luncheon Club contained a cross-section of the securities community was the consequence of the parlous times the club and the industry had endured thirty years earlier. In 1941, after a relentless squeeze on revenue resulting from the sluggish trading activity and nearly nonexistent underwriting, the club decided to open its door to "all classes of practitioners of the financial arts," not simply the carefully defined set of senior Exchange members that had previously been eligible. The pomp and snobbery of the club had gone, but it still bore the imprint of Wall Street's old guard.

Lewis often met people at the club, which was the microcosm of old Wall Street, where his father had become a millionaire and where the old man was still well remembered. If Lewis' plan came to fruition, he would have constructed a bridge between Wall Street's past and its future. Lewis seemed to consider this his personal challenge.

In contrast to the surrounding traditionalism, Lewis was a chronic adversary of the status quo. He liked to stir things up. "Life is a matter of rearranging pieces," he once said, and this was precisely what he had in mind for Shearson and American Express. Spurring change was his role in life. Lewis didn't much want to run a sprawling financial empire like Sandy Weill's; his satisfaction came from operating behind the scenes, where his impact ultimately was felt at Merrill Lynch, Dean Witter Reynolds, and other financial houses. He had the ability not only to disarm people, but, over time, to convince them of his logic. He tended to speak in long, stream-of-consciousness harangues, carrying his listener along on the flow of opinions, anecdotes, and reflections. By the time he returned to his starting point, he somehow would have made things look different from what they had seemed before. Lewis was also intensely personal in most of his business dealings. He was a financier who insisted on talking about feelings and emotions. And he viewed deals as dramas, preferably ones of which he was the director. He was fond of using literary comparisons to describe situations he encountered on Wall Street. Once, when the elderly chairman of a corporation seemed incapable of retiring from the business he'd spent his life building up, Lewis drew a comparison to King Lear, delving into the monarch's tragedy to explicate the problem of old men who are unable to let go.

Within the financial district, the mention of Sandy Lewis seldom brought a neutral reaction. Some people would recount incidents in which he had played the enfant terrible, disrupting otherwise orderly situations. Others simply found him impossible to get along with. But beyond this, people who knew Sandy Lewis on Wall Street or elsewhere depicted him as a sort of magus, a man who saw the world differently and who sought to change it to fit his own vision. His assaults on the status quo and his insistence on reordering things frequently antagonized those who found his style abrasive and his arrogance unpleasant, but many admired his intuition and vision. Sitting down to breakfast with Weill at the Luncheon

Club, Lewis presented, as both a recommendation and a prophecy, his idea of a single corporation that would offer many different financial services. Wall Street firms, he said, would someday be subsumed by companies that were bigger, perhaps blander, but vastly more rational and more sophisticated in marketing their services. What resulted wouldn't be just the brokerage business; it would be the money business. Lewis said this plan would help Weill lead the way into the new era: he was to sell his company to American Express.

Weill was stunned. After all, Lewis, five years his junior, was a virtual stranger. He seemed mercurial, brilliant perhaps, but not yet established. Weill dismissed the notion as outrageous. He wasn't used to an approach like Lewis', but he underestimated the younger man's capacity to change things, including Weill's own thinking.

Weill was a streetwise, cigar-chomping sort — one of the new breed of Wall Street empire-builders. He had launched his firm with three other partners in 1960 in a makeshift office at 15 Broad Street. In 1980, having swallowed up eight big securities houses, including Hayden Stone in 1970 and Loeb Rhoades Hornblower in 1979, Weill's firm employed 3388 stockbrokers. And Weill himself was a multimillionaire.

Shearson Loeb Rhoades was the second largest investment brokerage house when measured by total capital: the largest was Merrill Lynch. There were other respects in which Shearson came out number one: Shearson stock rose to $37.50 at the end of 1980, up 1960 percent from a year-end price of $1.82 a share in 1972 and up 257 percent from a year-end price of $10.50 in 1979. Merrill Lynch shares at the end of 1980 were $37.13, up 93 percent from $19.25 in 1979. The rise of Shearson's stock, in fact, surpassed that of any other publicly owned securities firm as measured on percentage basis. And although the firm was viewed as a Johnny-come-lately in the financial business, its net return on average equity — a widely accepted gauge of overall profitability — was the highest of any publicly traded securities firm.

Shearson, in a position to expect a steady increase in its total share of the securities market, was hardly a company in need of being acquired. It was inconceivable to Weill that Shearson could become the object of a takeover and that Weill himself would answer to another company's chairman.

Lewis, however, had been thinking of such a takeover for more than a decade. Beyond the appeal the merger held for him as a business concept, the role of making the merger between Shearson and American Express represented a success in his often turbulent life, a life that had been inevitably shaped, in one way or another, by the affairs of Wall Street.

Lewis' own firm, S. B. Lewis & Company, was in no sense a significant factor on the Street. It had been launched the previous May on about $8.4 million in partners' capital. One of the company's first objectives — privately discussed by Lewis with prospective partners before the formation of the company — was the merger he was now broaching to Weill. For its services as go-between, Sandy Lewis' firm would earn a hefty fee.

Making mergers happen had become a particularly lucrative pastime on Wall Street. The old-line investment banks, like Morgan Stanley, First Boston, Lehman Brothers, and Goldman Sachs — all companies involved in takeovers — were paid gargantuan fees, each a percentage of the dollar value of the entire transaction. "Deals" were the obsession. The top strategists of the takeover assaults — Robert Greenhill at Morgan Stanley, Joseph Perella and Bruce Wasserstein at First Boston, Ira Harris at Salomon Brothers — had become the stars of Wall Street, renowned for their often ingenious maneuvers in the merger arena. These men encouraged takeovers by using their considerable persuasive powers to prod corporation executives to swoop in on other companies.

And the action was heating up. There had been $44.3 billion worth of corporate mergers in 1980.

What was unusual about Sandy Lewis' effort was that it focused on Wall Street itself. Earlier, Wall Street merger tacticians focused on energy companies, publishing houses, or manufacturers. Initiating a merger of a Wall Street firm into a company outside the brokerage business could change the competitive balance in the securities business and make things tougher for the firms already operating on Wall Street. The other merger experts generally left their own industry alone. But Lewis seemed determined to remake Wall Street itself.

Despite his initial reaction to the merger idea, Weill was willing to listen. He was a chief executive who had never developed a sense of his own infallibility. In fact, he seemed constantly to be worrying that he was falling behind or missing an opportunity. Weill's admirers saw this quality as watchfulness: more than most, he was able to consider something new, they said. His detractors — and Weill had a number — said this trait stemmed from an abiding insecurity. Though he was successful, Weill carried the uneasy air of a kid from Brooklyn who didn't really feel he belonged in the prosperous station he had claimed for himself.

Weill had an unusual, complex appearance. He was a Jew, but his visage looked Egyptian; the line of his nose, extending from his forehead, lent him a pharaonic profile. He was heavyset, with a midriff that expanded when he was in the throes of a takeover, but he seemed feline, agile. His face went through sudden changes: when he grinned, he seemed warm and down to earth; then his mood might darken, his voice becoming hushed, his manner brooding.

Now, looking at him over the table, Lewis sensed that he responded to a certain amount of flattery. "You're the best, fastest-growing, and cleanest operation in the business," Lewis said. Then he presented the merger between Shearson and

American Express as a challenge for Weill; he was careful to play down any sense that it would be an act of selling-out. By characterizing the combination as a business challenge, Lewis knew he could make it impossible for Weill to dismiss.

Shearson, however excellent its record, was labeled as Wall Street's newcomer, but American Express had the prestige associated with America's corporate establishment. James D. Robinson III, the chairman and chief executive of American Express, was a polished corporate statesman whose demeanor, background, and reputation set him in another world from that of self-made Wall Street entrepreneurs like Weill. Though it celebrated its self-made millionaires, Wall Street obstinately denied them the cachet they most longed for. By becoming part of American Express, Weill could claim that distinction. The prospect was attractive.

Suddenly, the Shearson chief said, "The only way I'd do this is if I could be named president of American Express."

Now it was Lewis who backed off. "I doubt seriously that this will be a quid pro quo," he said. "It may happen, but it won't be promised." Then he smiled. He had hooked Weill on the idea, at least enough to make him explore the possibilities. "And I'll tell you something else," Lewis said. "I'll bet you're going to do this merger."

Lewis had begun his work as catalyst. Weill would view his life differently from the way he had before breakfast that morning. Not that he expected the merger to occur, but he had been moved a bit off center.

As Weill and Lewis left the club and walked outside, traders, brokers, clerks, and vendors spilled out of the subway and poured down the narrow streets like a stream, meandering here, eddying there, their faces blanched in the thin gray light.

Wall Street, crowded, sooty, and claustrophobic, was, in 1980, one of the remaining places where young people came to seek their fortunes. The securities business wasn't simply an industry where people worked and were well paid; it was a place of huge ambitions and huge rewards. Both loomed larger in relation to other careers in business.

But as an industry driven by personally ambitious entrepreneurs, it had its shortcomings. Many Wall Street companies were undermanaged. They functioned as loose congregations of deal-makers and traders, working to enlarge their commissions. There were also those who carried the entrepreneurial fervor too far; alongside the celebrated financiers of Wall Street were a certain number of people driven chiefly by greed. Insider trading, market manipulation, account-churning — frequent excesses of the money business — had always attracted those in search of a quick route to prosperity.

In terms of marketing services to the public, Wall Street stood woefully behind the rest of corporate America. Until the 1970s, securities firms had generally shunned consumer advertising, believing it to be better suited to selling detergents than encouraging investments. It wasn't until 1980 that Shearson, for example, bought its first television advertisement; it was an amateurish, ineffectual effort in which a man rose during a Shakespeare performance and blurted, "When the question is money, the answer is Shearson." The ad, created by Grey Advertising, was withdrawn within a year.

Companies like American Express possessed a far better understanding of these matters. Unlike Shearson, American Express had a recognizable identity among millions of Americans who were the sort of people Shearson and other securities firms wanted to do business with.

Lewis had already approached Jim Robinson with the idea of building a broad financial services' operation at American Express, beginning with the acquisition of Shearson. Several weeks before his breakfast with Weill, he met with Robinson and Alva Way, the de facto number two at American Express, for breakfast at the River Club on Manhattan's East Side, a sort of headquarters for Robinson and some other leaders of the WASP financial establishment. Robinson was still searching for a merger partner, having failed spectacularly in the clumsy attempt to grab McGraw-Hill in 1979. The publisher was a solid performer in the information business, and Robinson understandably viewed it as a nice catch for American Express. But he was wary of Lewis' idea: the securities business was risky. Lewis had suggested the notion of acquiring a securities firm to Robinson when the American Express chief was in the thick of the McGraw-Hill struggle. Robinson was cool to the idea of buying a securities firm then, and it seemed that he hadn't warmed to it over the intervening months. Firms produced raging profits when the markets were in vigorous shape, but those earnings shriveled when stock prices plunged and the volume of trading diminished. In the early 1970s, American Express had bought a 25 percent stake in Donaldson, Lufkin & Jenrette, which had been a successful Wall Street maverick in the 1960s. To the chagrin of American Express, the DLJ investment had deteriorated steadily in value, and eventually American Express unloaded the stock at a loss by distributing it to American Express shareholders as a special dividend.

Robinson and Lewis had worked together in the late 1960s at White Weld, a prestigious investment bank that, after a year of dwindling profits, was swallowed up by Merrill Lynch in 1978. When Lewis formed S. B. Lewis & Company in May 1980, he had succeeded in bringing in American Express as a limited partner. American Express had a special portfolio for such investments and put in about $4 million, vital for getting the new firm afloat. Initially, the firm's business was risk arbitrage, or speculating on takeover situations that often caused wild run-ups in stock prices. But once the company's trading efforts were under way, Lewis was ready to get to work on the merger of American Express and Shearson.

Until the idea became sufficiently attractive to Robinson and Weill, Lewis would have to pump the adrenaline the two chief executives seemed to lack. During the fall following his August breakfast, he regularly called both of them on the telephone to keep the notion alive: for Robinson, it would be a chance to buy an entrepreneurial outfit whose ability to make money was unsurpassed by any big brokerage house on Wall Street. For Weill, it would be the opportunity to ally himself with a firm that had prestige and marketing muscle. After a few failed efforts, Lewis succeeded in lining up an autumn lunch date for the two chief executives. It was to take place in the silvery American Express Tower at the foot of Broad Street.

The setting at American Express bespoke a corporate culture that seemed worlds away from the surrounding canyons of Wall Street. Securities houses, even the most staid, seemed in the grip of a frenzy. Traders and deal-makers lurched from one room to another, whooping over the latest jump in the market indices or the money supply numbers. Phones jangled constantly. At American Express, by contrast, there was an almost palpable hush. The long, carpeted corridors were sectioned off by doors. Lewis once said of the place, "I have a desire to holler over there." People seemed to be tucked away in closed offices. There were handsome paintings on the walls, but they lacked any human context: they occupied a corporate landscape emptied of any visible vitality.

Having spent hours imagining the meeting of the two men, Lewis was racing ahead of actual circumstance. Robinson and Weill were mildly interested, even a little intrigued, but Lewis was convinced that a merger would occur and that it would be a brilliant marriage of opposites, a fusion of established influence and entrepreneurial verve.

When Weill and Robinson met, each began sniffing out the

other. In some sense, each man was the other's missing piece: Robinson was the polished statesman Weill would probably never become on his own; Weill was an engine of entrepreneurial drive that Robinson couldn't himself emulate. The companies they ran reflected that difference.

At Shearson, there were no portraits of founding fathers, no broad public identification. But there were advantages to being unencumbered by history. When Shearson executives had new ideas, Weill would hear them out in his office as he paced in his shirt sleeves, one hand in his pants pocket, the other gripping a Te Amo cigar. Usually, the officials would get an answer before the end of the talk. By contrast, American Express sifted new ideas through a time-consuming committee process. The firm was plodding, cautious, and bureaucratic. Its ruling suite was populated by professional managers, not entrepreneurs. Shearson had a string of successful acquisitions behind it. American Express had fumbled repeatedly.

But American Express and its chairman were pure establishment. Robinson was the scion of an old banking dynasty in Georgia. Stocky, bright-eyed, impeccably groomed, he bore an unflappable sense of assurance. He had been in or around executive suites all during his career, and he seemed to belong there genetically. His career was adorned with a host of outside directorships and appointments to prestigious nonprofit boards. There was the Business Roundtable (the Vatican of corporate conservatism), Memorial Sloan-Kettering Hospital, and the Pilgrims of the United States.

But for the pronounced differences, there were reasons that the two companies might complement each other nicely. For instance, there were ways of combining the American Express charge cards — held by some twelve million people — with investment products at Shearson. During the lunch at American Express Tower, Lewis suggested that American Express and Shearson pursue a joint marketing venture without immediately tackling the trickier and more emotion-laden proposition of merging.

Lewis had another suggestion to offer. If eventually there was a merger of the two companies — as he believed there would be — the matchmaker would deserve to be paid. "I want your first fight to be over my fee," Lewis said. He asked Robinson and Weill to come back to him with a proposed fee in the event that a merger took place.

As it turned out, the Shearson chief was ambivalent about the matter of fee. Weill, inured to the lavish compensation practices of Wall Street, was comfortable with the premise that investment bankers' fees should be based on the size of the transaction, not the number of hours they worked on it. Fees for the multimillion-dollar mergers could run as high as $15 million. Still, Weill did not want to agree to a fee that might seem excessive. A merger of Shearson with American Express would carry a price tag of about $1 billion, so, under generally accepted practices, it wouldn't be out of line for Lewis to ask a fee of about $4 million. Weeks later, a maximum fee of $3.5 million was settled on. But neither Weill nor Robinson thought it all that likely that the fee would ever be paid.

Weill himself held about 450,000 of Shearson Loeb Rhoades common stock. If the American Express merger was completed, Weill stood to own about $30 million worth of American Express stock, roughly forty times the amount held by Robinson.

For Lewis, as has been noted, the merger was more than a business venture. (Indeed, he once told Robinson and Weill, half jokingly, that he might perform his matchmaker role for no fee, an idea he later dropped.) The fusion of Shearson and American Express was a turning point in the evolution of the financial business, but Robinson and Weill did not know, when the talks began, how important it was to Lewis himself.

2

People who came to know Sandy Lewis as a father, a financier, or a patron of various civic causes also came to know something of Sandy Lewis the child. He had a staunch belief in the premise that the child is father to the man, and he wanted others to appreciate that that was so, at least in his own case. Often, those who dealt with Lewis on Wall Street spent hours listening to him retell chapters of his personal history. However unconventional this seemed in the business world, it was often effective, because it enabled Lewis to sweep others into his own drama and hold them there. Even the uncomplimentary disclosures he made about himself enhanced his influence over people. When some reacted skittishly, Lewis took this as a signal that these people hadn't resolved problems of their own, and sometimes he would decide to avoid them.

Max Lewis, Sandy Lewis' grandfather, was born in 1864 in a village somewhere in the area long contested by Poland and Russia. At the age of nine, he immigrated to New York with his mother and father, who were fleeing the periodic persecutions visited on the Jewish communities in Eastern Europe. Shortly after arriving, Max's father, Salim, moved to Palestine.

Max and his mother found housing on Manhattan's Lower East Side, and the boy soon began to work in a cigarette factory.

When he was a young man, he met an American named Tom Lewis, who neither smoked nor drank, and to honor these abstentions, Max decided to adopt the name Lewis. He never divulged the European name he had shed.

Max Lewis, a tall, reserved, devout man, entered the garment business. In 1907, he married Hattie Lissner, whose family ran a dress company in Boston. The following year, they had a child, a boy whom they named Salim Lissner Lewis, after Max's father. A year and a half later, a girl was born; she was named Isabel, after Max's mother.

Although there were some financial strains, the family led a modest, respectable life in a floor-through apartment in Brookline. Salim was a bright boy who got consistently good marks in school, apparently with little effort. When he completed high school, he wanted to go to Harvard but was rejected. He enrolled in Boston University, where he was a star player on the football team, and on Saturdays he worked selling shoes. As a salesman, he was forceful, persuasive, and tireless.

After a year at Boston University, Salim dropped out and joined a quasi-professional football team in Boston. He earned $50 a week playing Saturday games and continued to earn money as a prodigious shoe salesman. According to one tale, Lewis once managed to sell a bereaved widow two pairs of alligator shoes for her deceased husband's burial. The widow had forgotten her husband's shoe size, so Salim convinced her to buy two pairs to be sure that one would fit.

But Lewis hated the shoe business and longed to land a job on Wall Street, which had become a place of fascination for him. During a trip to New York, he attended a party at the North Shore Country Club on Long Island. Outside the clubhouse, Lewis heard someone point out Herbert Salomon, who ran Salomon Brothers & Hutzler. Lewis rushed up, introduced himself, and said he was sure that he could do a fine job for him on Wall Street. It was difficult to say no to the huge, imposing, eager young man. So Salim Lewis soon had a job — as a runner making $17 a week. But in 1927, Wall Street was becoming the magical Golconda, where riches arrived effortlessly and where shoe salesmen became millionaires. Lewis was desperate to enter the feverish stock market.

After a short period, however, a Salomon partner told Lewis that his prospects for advancement at the firm were negligible, if not nonexistent. Lewis then obtained a job as a salesman at Barr Cohen, a small New York commission house. Soon, the frenzied excesses of the stock market bubble gave way to the Great Crash in 1929. Stocks, hugely inflated by investors' misguided belief in the upward pull of the market, plunged. The earlier prosperity was blown apart, and the stock market now battered those involved in it. Yet, as historians have pointed out, the financial disaster was worse for investors than for brokers. Lewis was certainly one who could weather the storm. He himself didn't have money to lose, and the calamitous conditions in the financial world created opportunities for newcomers to step in and pick up the pieces. In 1933, Lewis found a job at a little-known firm called Bear Stearns. The company, which wasn't much of a presence on Wall Street, had $800,000 in capital and about seventy-five employees.

The senior partners were uncertain of the company's direction, other than that it had to stay afloat in the treacherous times. Joseph Bear, remembered as everybody's "Uncle Joe," was a kind but ineffectual man. Robert Stearns was a tough, no-nonsense broker, but he wasn't as interested in expanding the firm as in husbanding his own capital. Theodore Low, another senior partner, was widely respected and considered "a gentleman to his fingertips." But he was innately cautious, and the economic dislocations of the Depression only deepened his wariness.

Lewis was a jolt to the firm. Later in his career, he was quoted as saying, "When problems came along, the bulk of people get very scared. That's when I like to play."

What Lewis liked to play, and a game in which he became one of the early masters, was arbitrage. This is a specialized type of trading in which returns are derived not so much from a gradual appreciation in value of the securities bought as from the sudden and often radical swing in value that may arise from a shift in external circumstances. Arbitrage involves a certain degree of magic. What is bought at one price one day may, under the right conditions, be sold at a vastly higher price soon after. A takeover, for example, can cause the shift; an acquirer is, as a rule, willing to pay a good deal more for a company than the marketplace reflects at any given time, often because, in the acquirer's eyes, the market is underpricing a security. Arbitrage is also a means of taking advantage of an artificial disparity in prices. If a particular stock is selling in London at $40 a share and in Hong Kong at $38, an arbitrageur can buy it in Hong Kong and sell in London at a profit without encountering any risk. The effect of this kind of play is to narrow or eliminate the disparity: the buyers in Hong Kong will drive up the stock price there, whereas the sellers in London will drive it down. This is how, it is believed, arbitrageurs make markets more efficient.

Lewis was given the task of creating a bond department for Bear Stearns and immediately found a chance to profit from the financial chaos. In the months between Roosevelt's election and his inauguration in the spring of 1933, the banks teetered on the edge of financial uncertainty. To meet the depositors' demands, banks either shut down completely or sold off bonds at fire-sale prices. Using Bear Stearns's money and borrowed funds, Lewis bought the cheap bonds and soon built up a hefty portfolio at the firm. With the enactment of the 1933 banking reform laws, the banks were largely shored up. Deposits up to specified limits were insured by the Federal Deposit Insurance Corporation. Financial confidence was restored, and over the ensuing months the banks became buyers of bonds. "I believed what President Roosevelt said," Lewis once said in an interview. "He said we were going to come out of this Depression via the easy-money route. Well, if you're going to come out of this Depression via the easy-money route, then bonds like Texas Corp's fives selling at seventy-five had to be stinking cheap; no question about that." Lewis had a visceral sense of the markets. Although he hadn't operated as a dealer in securities before, his instincts were usually sound.

In 1936, Salim met Diana Bonnor, a former model and actress and, at twenty-nine, a year older than Lewis. Like him, she was stong-willed; she was also stunning, stylish, and more worldly than he. At the time she was ending the second of two unsuccessful marriages. And in 1937, she married Salim Lewis.

The Lewises settled into a roomy apartment in the Buchanan, an apartment house at Forty-sixth Street and Third Avenue. The handsome and confident couple seemed the picture of success: he was a rising financier at Bear Stearns; she was an attractive wife who would enhance his career. On January 27, 1939, Diana Lewis gave birth to a boy at St.

Luke's Hospital in New York. (January 27 was also the birth date of Wolfgang Amadeus Mozart, a fact that Sandy Lewis frequently noted later.) He was named Salim Bonnor Lewis, but he was called Sandy.

In September 1940, the Lewises had another boy, whom they named Roger. As the boys grew older, Roger's presence became more difficult for Sandy. Roger was a beautiful child, with blond-red hair, round blue eyes, and an endearing expression. Sandy was a handsome child but was more solemn and tense than his younger brother. When Sandy was four, another baby brother was born, John Bonnor Lewis. With the three young children and a staff of servants, the apartment was full of commotion. But amidst all the activity, it was clear that Sandy was becoming an unhappy, even disturbed boy. At times he was isolated and unreachable; at others, he was wild and uncontrollable. In 1946, another Lewis child arrived. This was Diana Bonnor Lewis, a brown-eyed girl, who reminded everyone of her father. She was called Bonnie.

By the early 1940s, Salim Lewis had effectively taken control of Bear Stearns. While Teddy Low was away during the war, the partnership was left in Lewis' charge, and he expanded it aggressively. New traders were brought in, and he began making deals in railroad and utility businesses. Trading the masses of government bonds issued to support the war effort became another lucrative endeavor. Bear Stearns, located then at One Wall Street, was gaining notice within the financial world, mainly because of Lewis. By the time Teddy Low returned, the firm had grown from four partners to thirty, and Lewis, who had been nicknamed Cy, had captured control. In 1948, on his fortieth birthday, Lewis bragged to a friend, "If I never went downtown again, I'd do fine. I'd never have to earn another cent." But this was a course Cy Lewis would never willingly take.

Cy Lewis' huge physical presence and thundering voice

added to his impact. As he grew older and put on some weight, he became identified around Wall Street as the Bear in Bear Stearns. People liked the joke; some referred to the firm as "the Bear," and they meant Cy Lewis, who was alternately affectionate and snarling. After displacing Teddy Low as chief of the firm, Lewis lost respect for the older partner and often bullied him. He subjected others to similar treatment.

One story has it that Lewis kept a small army of Bear Stearns traders working the telephones after a fire alarm sounded in the building. Although the fire, which was on another floor, never spread, it did cripple the ventilation system, making the trading room unbearably hot. Lewis stared out into the room from a thronelike leatherback chair, and no trader left.

The tale is part of the Cy Lewis legend. The many stories about the Bear center on an unusually forceful man, with superb trading instincts and a desperate need to succeed. But the people closest to Cy Lewis remember him as being two men. One was a bold, swashbuckling figure who created a contagious sense of accomplishment in the financial world. The other was a troubled father and husband, confused by the problems that disrupted his family life. Lewis' own life would have been simpler if he had been driven merely by greed. But his quest for position on Wall Street was more complex; it had no natural stopping point, no resting place.

In the spring of 1949, Sandy Lewis' emotional problems became severe. Traditional school settings seemed to worsen his problems, and home life was increasingly turbulent. Cy and Diana finally acknowledged that special arrangements had to be made for their son. A business associate of Lewis' had a child who had been treated at the Sonia Sankman Orthogenic School in Chicago. It was a small institution that accepted only between thirty and thirty-five children at any one time, and was run by the Viennese-born Freudian psychologist Bruno Bettelheim. The school was associated with the University of Chicago and functioned both as a treatment center and a research facility where Dr. Bettelheim studied childhood emotional disorders. Sandy's parents decided that the Orthogenic School was the best choice for him.

A member of a wealthy Viennese family, Bruno Bettelheim had moved to the United States in 1939, after a year's imprisonment in the Nazi concentration camps Dachau and Buchenwald. Initially, he worked on a research project that involved the psychology of art education. (He had a doctorate in art history.) In 1944, he became the director of the Orthogenic School. The institution, begun about thirty years earlier, was an unremarkable place, lacking much success either in its treatment of emotionally disturbed children or in its research into child psychology. The University of Chicago had suggested that Dr. Bettelheim bring a new focus to the school or close it completely.

Dr. Bettelheim, who had devoted some time to the psychological effects of particular environments, looked on the school as a place in which to study the psychological effects of a carefully controlled environment. Immediately, he began to design what he considered to be a therapeutic milieu for the treatment of psychological disorders.

Dr. Bettelheim said he had noticed soon after coming to the school that children who made regular weekend visits to their homes would manifest on their return the problems that had brought them to the school in the first place. "Each Friday, kids would leave for long weekends at home, and the school's work would begin anew on Monday," he said. Under Dr. Bettelheim's regime, the children made only several short visits a year to their families; moreover, he would decide whether a child was emotionally ready to make such a trip. The shift sparked opposition both from parents, who didn't easily accept the implication that exposure to them worsened their children's problems, and from counselors who were forced to work through the weekend. The change, however, seemed to make life more predictable for the children.

In general, the school made every effort to meet most of each child's needs. The staff was constantly aware of the need for psychological security as well as material security. For example, Dr. Bettelheim insisted that snacks always be available. He believed that food carried, aside from nutriment, considerable symbolic import.

Dr. Bettelheim carefully selected children whose problems seemed to him strictly emotional. The enrollment of children who were retarded or who suffered from a physical handicap would have deflected the research objectives of the school. Since it was emotional disturbance that lay at the root of the children's problems, Dr. Bettelheim was tireless in his efforts to provide children with emotional security through a constellation of constructive relationships that would enable them to approach living differently from the way they had been doing. Bruno Bettelheim had experienced in the camps the horrors of a surrogate society dedicated to human annihilation. At the Orthogenic School, he sought to create a therapeutic milieu, an environment that affirmed the individuality of the confused, agitated, and lonely children who were brought there.

Dr. Bettelheim, known simply as Dr. B., was the center of the school. The guiding philosophy, the approach to handling children, and the discipline emanated from him. The counselors depended on him for advice in managing the sometimes wrenching aspects of their work. And many counselors were themselves in psychotherapy with Dr. Bettelheim.

Sandy Lewis arrived at the school on January 9, 1950, with

his parents. Located at 1365 East Sixtieth Street, at the edge of the University of Chicago campus, the Orthogenic School occupied a substantial brick house that had been the rectory of a church.

Sandy remained at the Orthogenic School for six and a half years. Academically, he progressed quickly, and through close work with Dr. Bettelheim and several of the school's counselors, he slowly began to emerge from his dark and unhappy childhood. Chicago became as much Sandy's orbit as New York had been, and when the question of college presented itself, he chose the University of Chicago.

Around the same time, he met Barbara Lisco, the daughter of a professor at the university, and in June 1960, the two were married. Academic work, it turned out, did not sustain Sandy's interest. He gradually fell behind in courses, and in 1963 began to serve as a counselor at the Orthogenic School, an involvement that held greater interest for him than college. Eventually, he dropped out of the university. At that point, he was pulled between two careers. One was psychology, the field of Bruno Bettelheim, his mentor. The other was Wall Street, the world where his father was a legendary figure. To Sandy, the latter was the more compelling of the two.

3

———

Sandy Lewis began his career on Wall Street where his father had begun his — at Salomon Brothers. He may have seemed to be following in his father's footsteps, but Sandy wasn't oblivious of the long shadow his father cast on Wall Street, and he had taken steps to move away from it. Working at Salomon Brothers was one such step — at least in Sandy's mind. Salomon had, after all, fired his father thirty-five years earlier, and to Sandy this meant the firm was not in his father's shadow. In addition, Cy Lewis, after some successful bond trading in the 1930s, had built his reputation by trading stocks. By contrast, Salomon, at the time Sandy Lewis joined, was principally a bond house.

When Sandy was interviewed by the Salomon partner John Gutfreund about a job at the firm, he made it clear that he wasn't interested in copying the pattern of his father, that is, building a successful Wall Street career at the expense of his family life. Gutfreund told him, "Don't worry. Everybody doesn't have to be Cy Lewis."

So Sandy began the job at the Chicago office of Salomon Brothers on March 16, 1964. In the summer of that year he moved with Barbara and their two little boys, Joshua and Jordan, to a rented house in South Orange, New Jersey, and commuted to 60 Wall Street, where he began a rigorous training program at the Salomon headquarters. Barbara kept busy in New Jersey and often took the boys to Cy and Diana Lewis' summer house in Elberon, New Jersey. It was a period of relative calm in the Lewis family, and when Barbara became pregnant again in the fall, everyone was pleased.

Salomon was an excellent place for Sandy Lewis to learn the intricacies of the securities markets. Founded in 1910 as a money broker, the firm had shunned the retail brokerage business and had operated as a power in the institutional markets, a path Goldman Sachs and Bear Stearns also took. More than any other house, Salomon stood at the nexus of the bond markets — trading municipal bonds, corporate debt, government securities. The firm was also moving more into stocks in the sixties. Lewis cycled through the company, sampling the trading operations and studying how each worked; then he began taking responsibility for his own group of institutional accounts.

The place intrigued him. "I like this," he once told Barbara when he came home from work. "It's the biggest equation I've ever played with. It makes chess look simple."

Lewis wanted to analyze Wall Street with the same zeal he had brought to understanding the logic of Bettelheim's Orthogenic School. Of course, Wall Street wasn't only a place to work; it was an element of his past, which he was equally intent on understanding. As a boy, he had been driven down by the chauffeur on Saturdays to see the trading rooms, where he sensed the pressures of having money at risk. Wall Street had always been a part of the family's life; it had provided the success, but it had also fueled his father's preoccupation with winning.

Wall Street seemed to be a whirlwind — people wanting to buy, people wanting to sell, most of all people wanting to become very rich. Money was the one measure of success on the Street, where wealth followed accomplishment more closely than in many other businesses. Even Wall Street professionals with relatively simple tastes attached great personal importance on their own net worth — this was the barometer. At the time Sandy Lewis got his start, many new players had joined the prosperity chase. Indeed, Wall Street was much changed from the days when Cy Lewis had arrived. The 1960s saw the big financial institutions take their place as the most important investors in the marketplace. The wholesale entry of bank trust departments, pension funds, mutual funds, and insurance companies meant an explosion of business for the firms that provided the brokerage services for these enormous players. Corporate pension funds, aided by liberating regulations in Washington, turned from their previous orientation to bonds and ventured into the bustling stock market, which had hitherto been considered too risky a place to invest retirement assets. Corporate noninsured pension assets invested in New York Stock Exchange securities swelled from $11.8 billion in 1959 to $46.5 billion in 1969. The mutual fund, suddenly a popular investment vehicle for individuals, became another large-scale player in the market. The funds, which held $16.8 billion in NYSE stocks in 1969, built up their holdings to $44.1 billion in 1969. Insurance companies went from $8.6 billion to $21.5 billion in the same period.

The growth in institutional holdings didn't mean only that

the various institutions held more stock; it meant also that the brokers had much more business. In 1960, three million shares changed hands on the New York Stock Exchange on an average day. In 1969, this was up to 11.4 million shares. In this same period, the number of individual stockbrokers grew from 27,896 to 52,466.

Another indication that the gold-rush mentality prevailed on Wall Street during the 1960s is that on October 29, 1968 — the thirty-ninth anniversary of Black Tuesday — a New York Stock Exchange membership, or seat, sold for $515,000, which remains a record.

The bounty was, ironically, built around a two-hundred-year-old pricing mechanism that amounted essentially to a cartel system. The New York Stock Exchange, which handled 90 percent of the trading business in the stocks it listed, set the minimum prices its members could charge for brokerage. The commissions varied according to the price of the stock and the size of the trade, but typically a brokerage firm would bring in about thirty-seven cents a share on the trades it handled. The fixed commission system and the levels established were geared to a stock market that individual investors, not institutions, dominated. When the institutions entered the market and paid at these same levels, the result was a bonanza for the brokers. For example, at thirty-seven cents a share, a 150,000-share trade by a big insurance company or pension fund would bring a brokerage fee of $55,500. Wall Street, under the fixed commission system, was one of the most lucrative clubs in the world. Members of the club were virtually guaranteed a share of the bounty.

New types of trading were needed to accommodate the gargantuan presence of the institutions. The auction on the floor of the New York Stock Exchange would be thrown into chaos if a broker arrived to sell, say, 800,000 shares of stock for a major institution, so a new block-trading system was devised, largely by Cy Lewis and Gustave Levy, the chief at Goldman Sachs. A securities firm would put together a block trade from "upstairs," the term for the firms' private trading rooms. The firm might take in the stock for its own account or find "the other side" among institutional clients. The profits could come in two ways. If Cy Lewis bought shares for Bear Stearns's account from an institutional client, the tiniest movement up in the stock would allow for big profits when Lewis later unloaded it. If Bear Stearns acted as agent and placed the shares with another institution, it would get the heaping brokerage commission. The firm would take the prearranged trade to the Exchange floor for formal execution and often would pick up individual customer orders that were awaiting execution.

The methods that brokerage firms employed to attract the institutional investor also were changing the business. Since, under the cartel pricing system, brokers didn't vie for business by chopping the price of brokerage, they turned to other means. Investment research, previously given short shrift on the Street, became an important business in itself. In 1959, three classmates from the Harvard Business School — William Donaldson, Dan Lufkin, and Richard Jenrette — formed their own firm, the first major research and institutional brokerage company. The three set as their goal removing the green eyeshade from the stock analyst, who previously had been relegated to gathering obscure statistics on publicly traded corporations. Once Donaldson, Lufkin & Jenrette and a host of other institutional research firms sprouted up, research became more thorough, perceptive, and intelligent. It was delivered to institutions, and, if they liked the ideas they read about, they could direct brokerage business to the firm that had done the research. Some of these arrangements were made formal through so-called soft-dollar agreements; that is, an institutional investor would agree to pay a broker a certain amount in brokerage commissions in exchange for research. Stock analysts indeed discarded their green eye-shades and became stars on Wall Street, commanding six-figure salaries and lavish bonuses if their advice brought in business from the institutions.

There were other blandishments to attract the institutions' brokerage business in the sixties. Institutional traders were entertained continually as brokers strained to lock in a portion of their brokerage business. The limousine companies were kept busy collecting institutional traders to take them to Madison Square Garden or to the best New York restaurants at the expense of one or another Wall Street firm. Investment seminars were frequently staged in Florida resorts or sunny islands; the institutional traders were the guests of the brokers who were eager for their business. One of the bosses at Salomon once showed a trader a packet of photos of New York call girls and asked him to procure any or all of them for a mutual fund operator whose patronage Salomon and other major firms were aggressively seeking.

Sandy Lewis became exasperated by the expectation that he would behave as his father did on Wall Street. He avoided the lavish entertainment circuit his father enjoyed and often criticized the mores of Wall Street. In some ways, of course, the two were similar. Sandy, aided by the advice and contacts of his father, proved to be an able trader, and like his father he became an unmistakable presence in the trading room — grabbing at telephones, smoking a cigar, shouting to other traders. But to people who spent any time around the younger Lewis, the differences were obvious. Sandy was still a product of Bruno Bettelheim's therapeutic environment. He tended to examine people's motives or feelings during the course of the day and to discuss them openly. Often, he challenged the ethics of his colleagues and frequently lambasted men who seemed to be neglecting their families or mishandling their children. Once, another Salomon trader became so angry with Lewis' running criticisms in the trading room that he suddenly socked him in the jaw.

Cy Lewis often urged his son to try adapting himself to the people he worked with. On one occasion, he cautioned, "Just remember where you were two years ago — in the ashcan." Sandy laughed and answered, "I don't think I was in the ashcan. I was working at Orthogenic."

Other explosive confrontations between Lewis and some Salomon traders were ignited by a bizarre trading practice known as "give-up." Lewis was rankled by the give-up system from the start. In its simplest configuration, it was a practice whereby an institution paid a brokerage firm a commission for services rendered and then directed that firm to give up some portion of the fee — sometimes as much as 90 percent — to another firm or other firms that had rendered services to the institution. The commissions fixed by the New York Stock Exchange were so inflated by then that firms didn't mind giving up even a sizable portion to somebody else.

Sandy was particularly opposed to issuing give-ups from fees for trades in which Salomon had acted as principal or had traded from its own inventory. Such requests often came from mutual fund operators, who wanted to send payments to retail firms like Bache or Merrill Lynch for distributing fund shares to individual investors.

Once, when asked by William Salomon to give up commissions under these terms, Sandy refused. According to one person who was in the Salomon trading room, Lewis stared at Billy Salomon in the heat of argument and then bellowed, "Go fuck yourself!" At this, the Salomon chief blanched and said, "If you ever say something like that again, you're fired." Lewis again stared at Salomon a few seconds and repeated, "Go fuck yourself." He wasn't fired — then.

Naturally, the reformer's zeal won him few friends. In 1967, Lewis objected to the trading activities of two of Salomon's men and insisted that Billy Salomon dismiss them. Sandy then left for a vacation; on his return he found the two traders still very much in place. Billy informed Lewis that he was the one being fired. Though William Simon, later Secretary of the Treasury, and other partners who admired Lewis protested, the decision stuck.

Elsewhere, Wall Street was "creaking open" to new players; the soaring markets and lavish incomes marked this period as the "go-go years." Money seemed to accumulate around personalities. David Meid, manager of the Winifield Growth Fund, helped stir up a fervid belief that the startling growth would never end. "The best way to preserve capital is to increase it," he was quoted as saying, and, indeed, his Winifield Growth Fund swelled to $270 million from $11 million in just two years. Bernie Cornfeld, once penniless and once a socialist, became the multimillionaire chief of Investors Overseas Services, a fund for European investors interested in riding the surge in American stocks. Part of Cornfeld's international investment program was the publicity surrounding his pleasure palace in the Alps and his celebrity-studded extravaganzas.

These were some of the better-known money managers of the go-go years, a new breed who made enormously lucrative careers of managing other people's money in vast batches. But the brokerage houses themselves were attracting scores of new participants, aggressive entrepreneurial types who were discovering that the stodgy and tradition-bound financial community was ready to reward newcomers.

One of these new arrivals was Sanford Weill, who was typical of the new breed in that he arrived without contacts on Wall Street or any credentials that qualified him for a career in finance. At the time Sandy came to the securities business, he lacked even a college degree.

Weill had grown up in the Bensonhurst section of Brooklyn, the son of Polish immigrants. Although some have attempted to portray him as the personification of rags-to-riches success, he didn't emerge from poverty; his was a reasonably secure middle-class background. His father was a successful dress manufacturer during most of Sandy's childhood. But Weill did come to Wall Street from a confusion of false starts, bad breaks, and dismal surprises.

In 1950, he had enrolled in Cornell University's engineering school, planning to study metallurgical engineering in preparation for entering the steel business, which his father had turned to from the dress business. Steel looked at the time like a profitable area. There was much talk about the aerospace program, and the universities were preparing people to take part in it.

Engineering at Cornell quickly proved to be much more difficult than Weill had expected. By Thanksgiving, he'd flunked out. Fortunately, there was a fall-back. Cornell had just created a probation status for students who had failed in one area of study but whom the university wanted to give a second chance before banishing them from the campus. Those relegated to this limbo status were labeled "unclassified students" and were monitored closely. In 1951, there were eleven students in this category, including Sandy Weill. Eventually, his grades improved, and Weill was allowed to transfer to a liberal arts program, where he decided to major in government. Weill, no academic, said he figured it was "a good bullshit major."

In April 1954, Sandy had a stroke of good luck. He reluctantly agreed to accept a blind date with a girl from Woodmere, Long Island. Joan Mosher, to Sandy's surprise, turned out to be a stunning brunette, bright and empathetic, the sort of girl who brought out the best of his own personality. There were more dates. After starting his senior year in college, Sandy asked Joan to marry him and she accepted.

Things seemed to be falling nicely into place. Sandy's grades had never been better, and he was eager to proceed with his life. Sandy and Joan planned their wedding for the week following his graduation, after which Sandy would serve a hitch with the Air Force and join his father in the steel-importing business. Meanwhile, Sandy had expanded his studies beyond the government major to include a series of courses in the business school at Cornell.

Life, however, had a way of tripping up Weill. In February of his senior year, the plans began to unravel. Sandy learned that his father intended to leave his mother for a younger woman. He rushed home to Brooklyn in an attempt to salvage the situation. Failing, he returned to college, badly shaken. The family rift also meant that his plans to enter the steel business were thrown off track. But the turmoil had only begun. A few months later, Sandy learned that a cost-accounting exam he had missed while he was in Brooklyn, trying to salvage his parents' marriage, had left him with insufficient credits for graduation.

He did take an exam in the subject and passed it, but by then it was too late for him to be awarded his diploma in June; he would have to wait until September. The delay cost him his stint with the Air Force and strengthened the doubts that Joan's parents had already voiced about their daughter's choice. A son-in-law without a diploma didn't exactly fit Paul Mosher's expectations. "Joan was a divine-looking girl," a family friend said. "He just felt she had better to choose from." That view was bluntly communicated to Sandy, but the wedding took place nonetheless — surrounded by tension.

After the wedding, Sandy began casting about for a job, but he found that the lack of a diploma made things difficult. One day, near Forty-first Street and Seventh Avenue, he noticed an office of the old securities firm of Bache & Company. He had never seen the inside of a brokerage office, and since the street window was darkly tinted to ensure that customers had privacy from passersby, he wandered in. What he saw was confusing: brokers picked up telephones, filled out slips, rushed back and forth across the room. Yet there was an undeniable surge of energy in the place that appealed to Weill. So he decided to add brokerage firms to the list of organizations he was canvassing for jobs. He had no luck at Bache. Nor at Merrill Lynch. Nor at Harris Upham. Finally Bear Stearns, Cy Lewis' firm, offered to pay him $150 a week as a runner. Sandy snapped up the opportunity.

Weill was still planning to enter the Air Force once he secured his diploma, so nothing seemed permanent. But several months later, when his sheepskin finally arrived, military needs were declining, and the Air Force was looking for excuses to turn down applicants. When Sandy took his physical at the Mitchell Air Force Base on Long Island, he failed because he had a tooth cavity. He went back to Bear Stearns to tell his boss he could have the cavity filled and go to Texas to flight school, or he could stay on with Bear Stearns, provided he got the necessary training to become a securities salesman. The company agreed, and the Air Force plan was jettisoned. At this point, the Weills were happy not to move. They had just learned that Joan was pregnant.

At Bear Stearns, Weill slowly built up a reasonable pool of brokerage clients, mostly Brooklyn merchants and professionals. After about a year, a job offer came from Burnham & Company, and Weill accepted it.

During his time at Bear Stearns, Weill had befriended a Wall Street arrival named Arthur Carter, who lived in a neighboring apartment in East Rockaway. Son of a lifelong employee of the United States Treasury Department, he had grown up in Woodmere, majored in French literature at Brown University, and often thought of becoming a pianist. After serving in the United States Coast Guard, however, Carter became set on entering the financial business and acquired a graduate degree in business from the Amos Tuck School in Hanover, New Hampshire. He then landed a job at Lehman Brothers, the investment bank. Weill and Carter regularly got together with their wives, and more often than not would talk about the stock business and the seemingly boundless opportunities it offered. Inevitably, they discussed the prospect of setting up their own securities firm.

The notion seemed overly adventurous to Weill. He possessed drive, but his ambitions were simple in those days. He used to tell Joan that he wanted to save up enough money to buy a deep fryer and a slide projector. Beyond this, she wasn't entirely sure what her husband wanted in the way of professional success.

Because Weill was skittish about risking his meager savings in a new securities firm, he and Carter decided to bring in at least one other participant. Carter got in touch with an old school friend from Woodmere, Roger Berlind.

Berlind was a tall, slender man with a clear, rosy look, horn-rimmed glasses, and wavy auburn hair. He had long wanted to write show tunes for Broadway, and after graduating from Princeton, an English major, he set out to compose songs at his parents' home, trekking into Manhattan to offer them to music publishers. Berlind tended to write witty, romantic tunes, which seemed out of date at a time when rock 'n roll music was taking hold. After a year and a half, without selling a single tune, Roger gave up the dream of being a songwriter and began a job search on Wall Street. Eastman Dillon, which was hiring new, inexperienced brokers, granted Berlind an interview. In some respects, Berlind seemed to be the antithesis of a stockbroker: he was introverted, soft-spoken, and had none of the usual attributes of a salesman. A test administered by Eastman Dillon to new applicants, Berlind later recalled, showed "that I was a nonstarter, a nerd, and that I had no economic motivation." Nonetheless, Berlind came across as unusually intelligent, and the firm decided to give him a try.

By the time Arthur Carter contacted him about launching a new firm, Berlind had developed a keen understanding of stock analysis and was one of Eastman Dillon's more successful young brokers. In fact, he was at the time talking with another Eastman Dillon broker, Peter Potoma, about setting up a new company.

So Berlind and Potoma joined forces with Carter and Weill. Each agreed to put in his net worth, and Berlind added a crucial ingredient in the form of a $40,000 loan from his mother. Each partner paid himself $12,000 a year. They opened for business as Carter, Berlind, Potoma & Weill on May 2, 1960, in a cramped office Burnham & Company rented to them at 15 Broad.

"There was a hysteria to doing business that wasn't my style and was a little frightening," Berlind recalled. Carter, who was the unquestioned chief in the firm, brought out a ledger book at the close of the trading day so that each partner could give an accounting of how much business he had done. The ritual continued, with permutations, for years to come.

The first departure — Peter Potoma's — came early and painfully. Peter, a bright, persuasive stockbroker, had an odd, unaccountable streak. He would disappear for several days, then return as though nothing had happened. The partners figured he was perhaps moving a little too fast and that he would eventually quiet down a bit. In the winter of 1962, they got a call from the surveillance office of the New York Stock Exchange. Peter's problems were graver than they had thought. There had been rumblings from some of the banks about a peculiar pattern that had shown up during the settling of trades by Potoma. An examination of Potoma's trading showed that he had been engaging in a pattern of free-riding, both in his account and his wife's, over which he had full discretion. The practice involved buying stock on its way up, but not paying for it. As the game is usually played, the buyer waits for a desired gain, then directs the clearing firm to sell the shares and keep the original purchase price. Thus, the free-rider is able to pocket the gain without putting up a dime. The practice violates the Big Board's rules, and it soon became clear that there would be disciplinary proceedings against Potoma.

For a new firm working to create a reputation on Wall Street, the news was devastating. Newcomers like Weill and Carter are often seen as gunslingers. When a founding partner is disciplined by the Big Board, that perception is engraved in stone. Anticipating the worst, Carter, Berlind, and Weill excised Potoma's name from the company before the Exchange announced its proceedings against him. On July 19, the Exchange's Board of Governors moved to suspend Potoma from any involvement with a member firm for a year. It was humiliating to have the first major mention of the company be the story that one of its original partners was being sidelined for regulatory violations. By the time the announcement hit the Dow Jones news ticker, the firm had become Carter, Berlind & Weill.

4

Carter worried that the taint of Potoma's rule violations would hamper the firm's ability to establish itself. Reputation was crucial in the financial world, where billions of dollars' worth of trades occurred daily on the basis of trust. There were transgressions at the most prominent firms, of course, but the prestige of the old-line houses would cover such problems as a sea closes over wrecked ships. Carter knew that for a firm lacking any history, the experience could be bad.

Despite the attention given the aggressive arrivals on Wall Street, the old powers still held sway in many respects. This was particularly true of the investment banks that managed corporate underwritings and other large financial transactions. Theirs was a world of hushed dignity, where wealth and influence resided with discreet, lordly financiers, and the old investment banks held the allegiance of America's biggest and best-known corporations. The investment banks hadn't expanded much into the business of trading big amounts of securities, the specialty of Bear Stearns and of Salomon. Nor had they set up big networks of retail branch offices, like Merrill Lynch and Bache. Instead, they advised corporations like IBM and Standard Oil of Ohio in the quiet opulence of their Wall Street offices; they structured their clients' financing strategies, negotiated their mergers or divestitures, and underwrote the securities offerings the corporations would make when they wished to raise funds in the marketplace.

The influence of the investment bankers was most apparent at syndicate meetings, in which the managing underwriters would summon together the bevy of firms interested in having a piece of an offering. If, say, Morgan Stanley was underwriting an issue of AT&T shares, it would form a syndicate consisting of dozens of other firms, which would agree to commit themselves to sell to investors varying portions of the offering. The old guard still dominated the syndicate meetings. A Morgan Stanley or Lehman Brothers partner would give the details of an offering to a roomful of syndicate experts from other houses, and they would be beholden to the managing underwriters for a piece of the offering.

Wall Street was ambivalent toward the notion of financial mobility: it rewarded the gutsy newcomers like Cy Lewis, but it steadfastly cherished the old guard and its aura of discretion. Around the partners' massive dining table at Lehman Brothers, where Robert Lehman ruled as a sort of benign despot, investment bankers were forbidden to use the word "deal" in discussing underwritings or mergers. The term was considered vulgar. An investment banker from Kuhn Loeb said of a partner from Salomon that he was a "barbarian," because he had called a corporate client of Kuhn Loeb's without first seeking his permission.

Dillon Read represented the old school perhaps more than

any other investment bank. One entered this prestigious financial house by stepping into a marbled vestibule, where a pink-cheeked elevator operator, wearing a beige jacket emblazoned with *D.R.*, waited to whisk one upstairs. The offices themselves resembled living rooms of Eastern gentry, with hunting prints, leather-bound editions of *Thoroughbreds I Have Known,* and, most prominently, stunning portraits of the firm's ancestral figures lining the wall — Clarence Dillon, James Forrestal, and C. Douglas Dillon. Any letter to one of the firm's corporate clients — which included such mainstays as Anheuser Busch, Superior Oil, and Tenneco — had to be inspected by one of the managing directors, who would make certain that a younger investment banker hadn't become too familiar or casual. Many of the investment bankers worked at dark rolltop desks reminiscent of the early part of the century. Yes, Wall Street provided a bonanza for the mavericks and off-beat financiers of the 1960s, but the old guard had hardly relinquished its power.

New personalities showed up at Carter, Berlind & Weill. In 1962, Arthur Levitt, Jr., arrived, after trying several careers. Like others in the early 1960s, he had gotten a whiff of opportunity from Wall Street. He was at the time an executive vice president of Oppenheimer Industries, a Kansas City–based cattle dealer. Before that, he had been a writer for the *Berkshire Eagle* and a promotion man with Time, Inc. Levitt had obvious drive, and though inexperienced in the securities business, he had definite presence. Tall, slender, with clear blue eyes and a wide, mobile mouth, he operated with a sense of assurance. His name, of course, was a prominent one in New York; his father, Arthur Levitt, Sr., was the perennial New York State comptroller.

"First, I didn't know of any business that I had seen or read about that had the diversity of the securities business,

and two, I didn't know of any business in America that allowed somebody to make the amount of money that the
securities business does," Levitt said later. His efforts to obtain a job at Salomon Brothers, A. G. Becker, and H. Hentz
were unavailing, but Carter, Berlind & Weill offered him a
start.

His one reservation in taking a job there was that the securities business, or at least Carter, Berlind & Weill, wasn't
just a job; it had to be a consuming passion, leaving little
room for other interests. The other thing that struck Levitt
immediately was that his new firm and its partners were
outlanders and upstarts in a business that valued heritage.
The firm's partners didn't seem to know the powerful and
prestigious people in the financial business.

And Wall Street cared about connections. Eugene Rottberg, treasurer of the World Bank, tells a story about visiting
Morgan Stanley in the early 1960s, when he was an attorney
with the Securities and Exchange Commission. He recalled
walking into a large room at the firm's headquarters and
seeing four men working at desks placed in the four corners
of the room. Rottberg introduced himself as an attorney with
the SEC who had come to New York to visit some of the
firms that the federal agency regulated. It was obvious that
this explanation was inadequate, but Rottberg was at a loss
as to what more he should say. Finally, one of the Morgan
partners asked, as discreetly as he could, "Yes, but who are
you?" Flustered, Rottberg added another shred of information about his role at the SEC, only to have the question
repeated. At last, the Morgan partner introduced himself,
gave his own name, paused, and added, "Princeton." He gave
the name of the partner to his right, and said, "Yale." Rottberg understood. "Brooklyn College," he replied.

In 1964, Marshall Cogan, one of the most headstrong and
combative deal-makers of the era, arrived at Carter, Berlind

& Weill, after having tried unsuccessfully to secure a job at Lehman Brothers and Goldman Sachs and after working briefly at the less prestigious Orvis Brothers.

One of Cogan's particular strengths was his understanding of the automobile business, in which there was considerable market action in the 1960s. To pay his way through the Harvard Business School, he had worked for a car dealership in Boston. There, he had gotten a feel for the auto business as a vast marketplace, changing according to patterns few were able to follow. Before joining Carter, Berlind & Weill, Cogan had developed a theory of how used-car prices could serve as a means for one to gauge future prices for new cars. He began to follow Chrysler closely and helped a number of big institutions get into the stock prior to its major turn-ups.

Cogan helped push Carter, Berlind & Weill into the deal-making business, advising corporations on mergers. He won considerable business for the firm from Charles Bludhorn, of Gulf & Western, and handled the company's partial tender offer for Allis-Chalmers in 1968. The firm handled three other major deals that year: Leasco's bid for Reliance Insurance, Great American Holding's bid for National General, and Curtis Publishing's bid for Downe Communications. Cogan gravitated toward the swashbuckling types outside the corporate main line and felt a particular affinity with the new conglomerate-makers.

Carter had also won a lot of corporate finance business, but mostly with unheard-of companies; the first corporate client was the Supreme Ribbon Company.

But the once tiny securities house of Carter, Berlind & Weill was adding staff steadily. In 1965, it had incorporated, because the corporation was a simpler structure from which to operate financially as it expanded. But like other Wall Street firms that made the same move, Carter, Berlind & Weill remained a partnership in spirit. The partners simply became the major shareholders in a private corporation. As a rule, they continued to think of themselves and refer to themselves as partners. Partnership was the classical Wall Street format and the modus operandi required by the New York Stock Exchange of all its members for decades. Efforts to allow a member firm to become a private corporation were fought, but a rule permitting the move was finally passed by a slender margin of the Exchange community in 1953. Even so, the Big Board required that those who owned stock in member firms "be actively engaged with the business of his member firm . . . and to devote the major portion of his time thereto." If "outsiders" — companies not in the securities business — were allowed to own portions of member firms, the power for the Exchange would be diluted substantially.

In 1967, Carter, Berlind & Weill made its first acquisition. It bought Bernstein Macauley. Arthur Levitt had a couple of connections there and knew that the thirty-four-year-old investment concern was willing to sell. The terms were agreed to with little dispute, and the deal sailed through. It wasn't a massively important step for Carter Berlind nor an overly complicated one. Bernstein Macauley was in the investment management business — separate from brokerage and underwritings — and could be run more or less autonomously as the portfolio management division of the securities firm. But it pointed to where the little firm was headed — growth through acquisition within the securities business.

By 1968, there was a heady sense of prosperity at the firm, but there were also deep tensions. Arthur Carter was beginning to sour on the brokerage business; he wanted to take the company in other directions. His thought was that it could become a merchant bank, providing advice and capital to companies in exchange for some direct ownership. Carter had also begun grousing that Berlind wasn't doing his share.

Then he complained about Weill, too. His solution was simple. He spoke with Levitt and Cogan separately and suggested a large reduction in Berlind's and Weill's levels of ownership. They could be chopped to, say, 1 percent each, a humiliating reduction that would certainly drive them away from the firm.

Levitt and Cogan felt uncomfortable about the plan. Cogan, though the latest arrival to the enterprise, argued that loyalty to the original partners should count for something. After several meetings with Kenneth Bialkin, an attorney with the prestigious New York law firm of Willkie, Farr & Gallagher, the partners decided that Carter was the one who should leave. The following day, Carter was gone. (Carter remembered his departure differently from the way his partners did. Twenty years after the fact, he conceded only that he had done sporadic grumbling about Weill and Berlind not pulling their weight, and he insisted that the parting of the ways was caused by a difference in attitude toward the firm's business approach.)

Carter then tried to persuade Cogan to join him in a new merchant banking venture, but Cogan stuck with the firm, which was adopting a new name and a new set of titles for the principal partners. It was decided that the company would be called Cogan, Berlind, Weill & Levitt and that in the reverse order of the names in the company name, the partners could choose their titles. This meant that Arthur Levitt was free to choose any title he wanted. Levitt wished to take control of the company, but fearful of being continually second-guessed by Cogan and Weill, he decided to take the safer path and become president. Weill then picked the title of chairman. Berlind, the least power-hungry, became the chief executive. The others promoted this partly because they thought of Berlind as a man they could shove around when they needed to. Cogan became the vice chairman, a vague title, surely, but he relished the fact that the firm began with his name.

In 1969, just after the realignment of Carter, Berlind & Weill into Cogan, Berlind, Weill & Levitt, the securities business hit problems. It was as though the frenetic excesses of the go-go years had bred their own restraint. A swarm of factors seemed to converge, bringing the glory days on Wall Street to a halt; economic problems and general discontent over the long and misguided military involvement in Southeast Asia produced a draining pessimism in the nation. Stock prices slid: on the New York Stock Exchange, an average share was worth $41.74 in 1969, down from $52.47 the previous year. Moreover, the record trading volume was creating strains, because it became obvious that many Wall Street firms were woefully ill equipped to process the business. Wall Street was, by and large, managed by salesmen, gregarious men who knew how to sell stocks and how to motivate others to sell. They were not, as a rule, much interested in the complicated functions of the "back office," where the business was processed, nor were they disposed to invest in the computers, management, and planning efforts needed to ensure a smooth handling of the paperwork.

Securities firms were experiencing digestion problems. The Exchange began closing the floor on Wednesdays and shutting down trading at two-thirty on certain days to contain the volume. Members were called in on Saturdays to handle the crush of paper. Then a member firm — Pickard & Company — failed because of losses related to paperwork snarls. Others began flailing about in the confusion.

Companies that cleared for a host of smaller firms were feeling an overload. Burnham & Company began an examination of its clearing business and discovered an oddity: Cogan, Berlind, Weill & Levitt represented a huge portion of the business Burnham & Company processed each day. I. W.

Burnham, generally known as Tubby for his considerable girth, decided it was time to talk things out with the partners of the aggressive new firm. Things proceeded badly at a dinner meeting. To Cogan, Burnham represented the imperious old guard. For his part, Cogan came off as too impetuous and headstrong. The following morning, Burnham called to say that the clearing relationship was over; the firm would have to fend for itself.

It was a devastating blow and intensified the partners' feelings of being parvenus on Wall Street. As CBWL launched its campaign to find another clearinghouse, the partners decided to approach one of the most venerated patricians of the financial world, John Loeb, chief of the highly respected Loeb Rhoades. Loeb, however, said clearing arrangements with CBWL would be impossible: taking in a firm doing such an active business would strain Loeb Rhoades's capacity. Given the problems many firms were having with the trading volume, the explanation was perfectly plausible. But it was seen at CBWL as another instance of old Wall Street telling the upstarts that they were moving too fast, that they weren't doing things just the way they should. John Loeb was known for his insistence on doing business of only the highest quality and propriety. CBWL then turned to Lehman Brothers in hopes of establishing a correspondent clearing relationship there. Again, the partners were rebuffed.

They were understandably quaking at the task of setting up their own processing facilities, in part because the rest of Wall Street seemed to have handled it so ineptly. In addition, the change would create new economic criteria for the company. Before, it had paid Burnham & Company a fee for the business it cleared there. When volume turned down and brokerage commissions dried up, its clearing costs plunged as well. And when volume increases meant a jump in clearing costs, there would be large commissions to meet the expense.

As a self-clearing firm, CBWL would have a considerable fixed cost that it would have to cover. Volume might dry up, but the firm would still have to bear the personnel costs of its operations department and shell out funds for computer leases.

Yet Burnham's decision ultimately had the effect of starting Cogan, Berlind, Weill & Levitt on its way to being a Wall Street giant. The company had a distinct advantage in that it was starting from scratch. It didn't have to make the mistakes the others had made over the years. It could build an operations system that represented the state-of-the-art in data-processing technology. Weill got involved in building the back office, and the firm had hired Frank Zarb, a Brooklyn-born operations expert from Goodbody & Company, and later the Secretary of Energy, to oversee the project.

The investment in a gleaming new back office, of course, meant that the company would need enough daily volume to justify it. This meant, in turn, that CBWL would have to increase orders from individual investors; Weill was convinced that this made sense when he saw that the huge profits from institutional brokerage were almost gone. The signs were clear enough. In 1968, the Securities and Exchange Commission had outlawed the give-up, and now the Justice Department was raising questions about the fixed-rate system and was pushing the SEC to go farther in its inquiries. The cartel system, whereby the New York Stock Exchange set prices for the industry, was clearly under attack.

Taking apart that system turned out to be an arduous task, but it was accomplished. In 1971, the Exchange agreed that brokers and their customers could negotiate a brokerage rate for the portion of a block valued over $500,000. In 1975, after desperate opposition from Wall Street's old guard, Congress unfixed commissions for all brokerage.

But once again fate seemed to trip Weill and his partners.

Individuals weren't rushing toward the market; the slump of 1969 was followed by a stock plunge in 1970. The Dow Jones Industrial Average began that year at about 800, down some 15 percent from a year earlier. But the bellwether market average then entered a sickening slide, ending in January at a three-year low of 744. Wall Street was conditioned to expect ups and downs, but things seemed unseasonably bad in 1970. By March, amid declining revenue on a shrinking capital base, McDonnell & Company glumly announced that it would close its doors. It was a prestigious old firm that had enjoyed the allegiance of the Ford and the Kennedy families. Cogan, Berlind, Weill & Levitt snapped up the firm's Beverly Hills office in an effort to add a trickle of brokerage commissions to its meager intake, but it didn't produce much revenue. And other brokerage firms were tumbling into the abyss. Baerwald & DeBoer and Kleiner Bell, both lesser names, shut down around the time of the McDonnell failure.

The malaise extended far beyond Wall Street. The spring of 1970 offered up to the nation the ugliness of the United States' invasion of Cambodia and the shooting of American students at Kent State. Neither event was in itself "financial," but both took a dreadful toll on the nation's spirit. Shocked and sickened, people were not disposed to invest money in the future of the country.

On May 25, the Dow Jones Industrial Average sank 20.81 points, closing just above 640. It was the largest drop for any single day since the assassination of President Kennedy in 1963. Then, in June, the nation's financial miseries deepened when the Penn Central Transportation Corporation suddenly went bankrupt. Short-term credit markets were threatened with chaos, but the Federal Reserve Board managed to avert a panic by initiating a liberal lending policy.

What followed in the next several months constitutes one of the more bizarre dramas on Wall Street. But it had the consequence of providing Weill and his partners with their power base. During the summer, concern was beginning to center on what was a growing problem within the financial community. This was the emergence of grave financial problems at one of the oldest and largest securities firms — Hayden Stone. The seventy-eight-year-old company was where Joseph Kennedy had built much of his fortune in the 1920s. It had a solid investment banking business, having underwritten securities offerings for such companies as Kennecott and International Nickel. Hayden Stone had a network of about eighty branches and some ninety thousand customers. And it had enormous problems. The firm had been all but submerged in paperwork errors in 1968. Its remedy was an expensive and somewhat awkward positioning of modern computers on an outmoded and archaic foundation. In 1969, the firm lost about $5 million, a large sum for those days. By the start of 1970, it had shrunk its branch system to sixty-two offices and continued to lose money at an accelerating rate.

The prospect of Hayden Stone's going under was a ghastly one. Wall Street firms were partnerships, and the NYSE was essentially a partnership of partnerships. That means that the weakest would drag down others. The New York Stock Exchange operated a Special Trust Fund, financed by its members, to make whole investors harmed by the failure of a member firm. But this fund was already being drained by the steady flow of Wall Street failures, and even in the best of times it wasn't capitalized at a level that could possibly accommodate the collapse of a company as large as Hayden Stone.

In March 1970, the beleaguered firm found an unlikely champion. Far from the financial enclave, it was a consortium of hard-boiled Oklahoma businessmen, who agreed, on Friday, March 13, to put $12.4 million in stocks into the firm in return for "demand notes" from Hayden Stone. The group was an odd rescue team for a Wall Street dowager in distress. There was Bill Swisher, who ran CMI Corporation, which made road-construction equipment; Jack Clark, the chief of Four Seasons Nursing Centers; there were a number of executives and shareholders of Woods Corporation, which was involved in trucking and prefabricated buildings; there was the company of IHC, Inc., which made electric machinery and stretch wigs. Jack Golsen, chairman of LSB Industries, Inc., a maker of bearings, tools, and air conditioners, was also part of the deal.

The financial arrangement was by most business standards an unusual one, though not by comparison with some of the queer accounting games played on Wall Street. The Oklahomans would deliver to Hayden Stone stock they owned, most of it in the companies they ran. These shares, lent to the firm, would be counted as part of Hayden Stone's capital. The firm would then have to meet a slew of financial requirements of the Big Board and the Securities and Exchange Commission. With more capital to offset liabilities, Hayden Stone could proceed with plans to expand and thereby bring in more revenue to cover what had become a costly operation. The Oklahomans would receive an effective interest rate of 7 percent, which was highly attractive then, and they would also receive options to buy Hayden Stone stock.

When the offering circular presented to the Oklahomans had been perused a few months earlier at the New York Stock Exchange, Robert M. Bishop, a vice president, had posed a series of questions to Hayden Stone. The import of them was the suggestion that the firm was painting too rosy a picture of itself. Nonetheless, the document, unaltered, was presented to the Oklahoma investors.

About a month after the agreement was signed, Jack Golsen found himself with a free afternoon in New York, and he telephoned Hayden Stone's offices to say he'd like to drop by. The response was somewhat troubling: it wouldn't be at all convenient, because an executive committee meeting was in progress. Golsen wondered what was being discussed at the executive committee meeting that he, who had put up nearly $1 million in LSB securities, wasn't entitled to hear. Golsen took a taxi to Hayden Stone's office. Several executives of the firm bustled out to suggest that he come the following day.

Golsen, feet planted, said that was impossible. "No, I'll sit here just as quiet as a mouse," he added.

The company could hardly call the police to eject him. Golsen, as promised, seated himself on the side of the room. Things seemed very different from the way they had a month earlier, when the agreement was signed in Oklahoma. In contrast to the breezily confident presentation that led up to the Friday-the-thirteenth agreement, there was an air of consternation. January's financial results, which had been favorably described in March to the investors, were, in fact, clouded by a large number of items.

Golsen felt a sense of outrage; he wanted a full audit. Later, at a meeting in Oklahoma with the other investors, he also pushed for a watchdog to work with Hayden Stone on behalf of the group. This was to be Larry Hartzog, a lawyer for Woods Corporation.

Hartzog flew to New York to size things up. One option, of course, was to sue Hayden Stone, along with Donald Stroben, its executive vice president, and Alfred J. Coyle, its chief executive. But with more than $12 million tied up in the firm, the Oklahomans were loath to bludgeon it with litigation. They decided that a better course would be to help the firm make a comeback. Perhaps a management change would help. The rescue team anointed the forty-year-old Stroben as chairman and chief executive and demoted the forty-nine-year-old Coyle to the chairmanship of the executive committee. Then there would have to be radical cost-cutting. This time, they would tap the previously untouched and sacred executive salaries and bonuses. Even so, the financial details of the company seemed boggling. There was a deep, enraging irony to the whole mess, as Golsen saw it: Wall Street, which held itself out to corporate America as the bastion of financial wisdom, had left its own financial structures in confusion. The entire scaffolding of Hayden Stone seemed to teeter. Assets appeared and disappeared. For example, it turned out that the firm carried about $7 million in what was known as "short differences." These were securities that, according to the records, should have been in Hayden Stone's vaults, but that, for no particular reason, weren't. No one at the firm would say just why; no one offered any suggestions as to how the paper might be recovered. Golsen knew of few businesses that managed their inventories in so casual a fashion. In the meantime, losses worsened. For March 1970, the firm posted a thumping after-tax debit of almost $700,000.

Even the infusion of assets from Oklahoma was somewhat shaky. Hayden Stone was vulnerable to the ups and downs of the companies whose stock had been put up and counted as Hayden Stone capital. The shakiness of such an arrangement became clear on May 13, when the Securities and Exchange Commission suspended trading in one of the stocks put up, the Four Seasons Nursing Centers. This company's own finances had slipped into a morass, and soon after the trading halt it declared bankruptcy, ruining the value of the Four Seasons securities in Hayden Stone's vaults and deepening the firm's financial chaos.

June brought an even more calamitous development. Haskins & Sells, the big accountant, performed an audit that showed a dismal erosion of Hayden Stone's capital position.

One immediate upshot was that the company found itself in violation of the New York Stock Exchange capital requirements. The Big Board moved to establish a strict timetable for the firm. "You are hereby directed to prepare a plan and submit it to the Exchange by 10:00 A.M. on Wednesday, June 24, 1970, which will show how you will return to capital compliance by Monday, June 29," the Big Board said in a communiqué to Stroben.

Hayden Stone then embarked on a series of Draconian steps to raise cash. It shed underwriting agreements, which created liabilities. It sold off securities accumulated from other underwritings. It liquidated securities collateralizing loans made by subordinated lenders. These were painful steps — and they left the company still short of the funds it needed. So Hayden Stone turned to the Exchange itself for succor. The Special Trust Fund was, though not robust, intact, and the Exchange went along with the plan to aid the failing firm. In other businesses, a company run as badly as Hayden Stone would have been forced to live with the consequences of its mismanagement. On Wall Street, the Big Board acted paternalistically to help firms from going down.

The Exchange decided that Hayden Stone's only hope lay in merging with a healthy securities firm. Some of the better-known Wall Street names were brought into the discussion — Bache & Company, Reynolds & Company, Shearson Hammill, and Walston & Company.

In early August, Hayston Stone called its 108 subordinated lenders to a meeting at the prestigious New York Racquet and Tennis Club on Park Avenue. Not all of them knew the extent of Hayden Stone's problems. Lee Arnings, a vice president of the Exchange, explained to the group that if Hayden Stone wasn't absorbed soon by another company, the probable outcome would be the firm's suspension from the Exchange. Some of those in attendance were stunned by how bad things had become. Jack Golsen once again grew blistering mad that the firm had conducted its affairs so badly.

The absence of a willing partner for the company opened an opportunity for a lesser-known firm that had been sniffing hungrily around the edges of the disaster: Cogan, Berlind, Weill & Levitt. The day after the Racquet Club meeting, Larry Hartzog, the Oklahoma lawyer, began talking with the CBWL partners about a merger plan. Some of the Wall Street establishment had barely heard of the firm. Its initials were jokingly said to stand for Corned Beef With Lettuce. There was another incongruity: Hayden Stone was many times larger than the firm that proposed to absorb it.

But there were plusses. CBWL was in sound financial condition, compared with others on Wall Street, and its operational system was of a caliber that instilled some confidence that the merger would occur smoothly. There was another element on the side of the merger: Cogan and Weill were becoming fierce in their determination to do the deal, and both were difficult men to dissuade. It would, after all, vault the company in one leap into the ranks of sizable retail brokers, and it would provide it with the flow of orders needed to cover its unyielding operations costs. Cogan began to push for the deal with a determination that bordered on obsession. "We need the legitimacy of history," he said repeatedly. He also told a friend, not entirely in jest, "It's either do the Hayden Stone deal or close down."

As the talks went on, it was tentatively decided that CBWL would acquire about twenty of the forty-five Hayden Stone offices that were still open after the last round of cutbacks. What was most significant was that CBWL would gain the Hayden Stone name. A shell company, HS Equities, would be established to wind down open transactions involving Hayden Stone. In this way, CBWL wouldn't be acquiring any of the firm's problems. It would gain offices, revenue, and a $6 million capital contribution from Hayden Stone.

Limousines carrying retired Hayden Stone partners and widows of partners arrived for a second meeting at the Racquet Club. Berlind, as CBWL's chief executive, explained to all assembled the outlines of the proposed acquisition; additional comments were made by David Stone, grandson of one of the company's founders and a shareholder himself. The subordinated lenders would receive preferred stock in HS Equities, which, in turn, would receive debentures, common stock, and warrants from the new company, to be called CBWL–Hayden Stone. One peculiarity of the deal was that the Exchange Special Trust Fund, as one of the subordinated lenders to Hayden Stone, would effectively become a shareholder in one of its member firms. However, the rescue effort seemed sufficiently important to permit a few irregularities.

But a bolt from the Midwest almost struck down the fragile edifice. The Chicago Board of Trade, concluding that Hayden Stone lay perilously close to insolvency, had insisted that the firm transfer all its customer accounts to other firms — within two days. The Stock Exchange was conscripted to cajole more time from Chicago. By now, the Exchange had established a crisis committee, co-chaired by the Big Board chairman Bernard (Bunny) Lasker, a prominent Exchange market-maker and an avid Wall Street ally of Richard Nixon, and Felix Rohatyn, the Vienna-born partner at Lazard Frères. They managed to hold off the ultimatum from the Board of Trade so that there was time for the CBWL deal to be completed.

For the merger plan to go through, the blessing of all 108 subordinated lenders was needed, ensuring that none of them would, in anger, sue CBWL after the acquisition. The merger plan had been described in some detail at the second Racquet Club meeting, and most of the Hayden Stone lenders had signed agreements then and there. Jack Golsen, however, announced that he had no intention of signing any agreement until every other subordinated lender had done so. A few others resisted as well, but they were convinced when the Exchange crisis committee presented it as a matter of solemn urgency: it wasn't simply Hayden Stone; it was the entire financial system that was at stake. If Hayden Stone went under, the Special Trust Fund couldn't possibly rescue the firm's helpless customers. There would be a staggering loss of confidence, and investors would pull their accounts away from Wall Street. As a result, other firms would go under, leaving more customers empty-handed. In the end, as many as two hundred securities firms might collapse.

The Exchange set a hard deadline: the deal had to be in place by noon, Thursday, September 10. The lenders were thus forced to make a decision, and given the possibly dire consequences of scotching the merger, they signed. On September 10, only Golsen was left. Assuming that he would agree, the Exchange cheerfully telephoned him to inform him of the status of things. About an hour short of the noontime deadline, Golsen's lawyer, Michael Yamin, called back to say that his client would not sign the agreement and that he wasn't available to discuss the matter, since he was in Texas on business. The Exchange's Board of Governors scrambled to extend the deadline until ten o'clock the following morning.

There was general disbelief that Golsen was going to stand in the way of the merger. Felix Rohatyn called Golsen's lawyer and was told that Golsen believed he had been baldly defrauded on his Hayden Stone investment and that the Exchange was moving in to paper over the entire mess.

Cogan insisted on flying immediately to Oklahoma; he was determined to clear away this last roadblock to the firm's move. He chartered a Learjet at the Teterboro Airport in New Jersey. Berlind, David Stone, and Larry Hartzog accompanied him, each rehearsing the various arguments he would use to convince the last holdout to sign the agreement. The night was foggy and wet, and the negotiators were stranded for hours at the airport, from which they made repeated telephone calls to New York and Oklahoma City. Weill, Levitt, Kenneth Bialkin (serving as CBWL's attorney), and Rohatyn were stationed at different points in New York. Bunny Lasker was at his suite at the Carlyle for much of the crisis committee's tenure.

Finally, the weather improved sufficiently for the Learjet to take off. When the plane arrived in Oklahoma, it was close to 4:00 A.M. Cogan insisted on stopping for coffee before meeting Golsen, who had been located and had agreed to meet the New York delegation at his office. The offices of Golsen's LSB Industries were the typical bland, anonymous business setting. In a workable conference room, the men settled down for what would be a protracted faceoff. Cogan assumed the lead debater's role with the fervor he had expressed earlier when persuading the others to go along with the merger. First he went through the reasons that had been used to convert the other holdouts: it wasn't simply a matter of saving Hayden Stone; there could well be a crisis of confidence if the firm collapsed. Other securities houses would fold; thousands of investors would be ruined. Wall Street, brought to its knees, might be taken over by the banks or perhaps managed by the government as a public utility. This litany had been sufficient to win over the other lenders. But Golsen, who by then had written off his Wall Street investment as a total loss, had no hope that its value would be revived through a merger with CBWL. He felt that he was a man defrauded and that it was unjust for the perpetrators to be bailed out.

Cogan was stymied. Others came to press that Hayden Stone not be allowed to slide into oblivion. Bill Swisher, the chief of CMI Corporation and a fellow victim of the debacle, was flown in from Chicago. Alan Greenberg, a top trader at Bear Stearns and himself an Oklahoma native, had telegraphed Golsen, a school friend from years before, and urged that he sign. Then the heavy artillery was wheeled out. Wall Street leaders — if they were sleeping at all back in New York — were awakened to talk to Golsen over the telephone. Golsen's suppliers of trucks were jangled awake and asked to speak on behalf of the deal. Most vociferous of all was Bunny Lasker, who had seen his own fortunes swell on Wall Street and who was agonized by the prospects of a Wall Street calamity. Lasker had one card left to play: Richard Nixon had long said he was in Lasker's debt, because the Wall Street market-maker had persuaded him to stay clear of the presidential elections in 1964. Lasker had been in touch with aides at the White House that day. With the standoff seemingly unresolvable, Lasker called Golsen to say that the President was standing by and he'd soon have him on the line. "No," said the Oklahoman. "I won't take the call."

Back in New York, Weill and Levitt were witless with nerves. A wracked congregation of floor brokers, market-makers, and traders began milling tensely around the Big Board, waiting for the trading to begin, not knowing just what would unfold. It was nine-thirty New York time, half an hour before Hayden Stone was to be suspended.

In Oklahoma, the standoff continued. Cogan looked across the conference table at Golsen.

"Jack, can we go into your office?" he asked. "I want to speak with you alone."

Golsen assented. He and Cogan, both exhausted, raw-edged, stepped into the adjacent office and closed the door.

"Jack," Cogan began, "you're a Jew. So am I. We both know what discrimination is because we've both experienced it." The two men sat still for a few moments; Golsen said nothing. Then Cogan went on. "If this deal falls through, and if there's a disaster, the story that's going to go around is that 'a tough Jew brought down Wall Street.' I know it and you know it, Jack. Don't do this to the American Jewry.''

Five minutes later, Cogan streaked out of the little office, past Berlind, Stone, and the lawyers and aides. He grabbed the telephone to call Alex Chapro, CBWL's shrewd floor partner on the Big Board and a man to whom Cogan was indebted for his adept handling of the stream of orders during the institutional heyday of the 1960s. It took a few minutes to get through. Shortly afterward, there was a cheer on the floor of the New York Stock Exchange — not a single burst, but a sort of slow, expanding roar. The deal was done, and a new firm was in business — CBWL–Hayden Stone. Chapro and his team of CBWL brokers were ready for business with a sheaf of order tickets carrying the new name emblazoned at the top.

5

William Simon thought Sandy Lewis was one of the most brilliant people to have worked at Salomon Brothers, and he was disappointed at the failure of his efforts to salvage Lewis' job. In March 1967 Simon helped secure Lewis a post at White Weld, a seventy-two-year-old investment banking firm, which was beefing up its securities trading activities.

As at Salomon Brothers, Lewis at once became a controversial presence. He was fascinated by the varied movements of stocks but was contemptuous of the practices that went along with attracting the business of the institutional money managers. For example, he steadfastly refused to have Barbara entertain his business clients. Reared as a professor's daughter, she had simple tastes and little interest in the expense-account life that flourished around Wall Street. She preferred playing the piano or reading in her spare time, which was spare enough, since the Lewises, by this time, had had their third child, a girl whom they named Kari, after a counselor at the Orthogenic School.

Lewis not only saw things differently from the people around him but sought opportunities to describe his own perspective. At White Weld, he once stunned onlookers when he explained to a powerful trader with a big New York bank that, unlike others on Wall Street, he had no intention of wining and dining him in hopes of attracting his brokerage commissions. "It's very simple," Lewis told the banker in a clipped, staccato voice. "I will never so much as buy you a cup of coffee. I wish to perform for the clients of the firm, and if I don't, I'd like to hear from you."

The banker did send a significant portion of his business to Lewis, it turned out, but only because he liked the way Lewis traded stocks. Other clients weren't used to the straight talk they got from the young trader; they found him abrasive. One former White Weld partner recalled, "There were two kinds of clients at White Weld: those who would speak to Lewis and those who wouldn't." Some White Weld partners also clashed with Lewis.

One of the bankers Lewis worked with at White Weld was James D. Robinson III. He fitted the stereotype of a WASP investment man in only some respects: he was immaculately tailored, scrubbed, and consummately respectable. Born to a prominent family in Atlanta, where his father and grandfather had been chairmen of the First National Bank of Atlanta, he graduated from the Harvard Business School and progressed to what seemed the next natural state of ascendency — the Morgan Guaranty Bank. Eventually, he became the special assistant to the Morgan chairman, Thomas Gates. Robinson was comfortable in these spheres; he belonged. But in other respects Lewis found Robinson to be different from some bankers he had brushed up against at White Weld. Robinson was pinstriped and respectable without being stuffy. He seemed friendly, straightforward, and decent, without a trace of snobbery. His friendship and that of several others at the firm provided Lewis with needed contact at a time then he felt increasingly isolated.

Over New Year's of 1969–1970, Sandy joined his father and Gus Levy of Goldman Sachs for a respite in Acapulco. Also along on the trip was a long-time client of Goldman Sachs, Arthur M. Wood, the chief executive of Sears Roebuck. Lewis and Levy were lamenting what seemed to be the end of the days of glory in the institutional business on Wall Street. Washington was becoming too reform-minded, they felt, and was about to ruin a good thing. And the once high-stepping stock business seemed to be in the doldrums.

Sandy Lewis listened, somewhat bemused, and then offered his own conclusion — that the Wall Street business was headed toward a massive shakeout and that in the next decade financial services would be delivered in entirely new formats. He suggested that someday Sears Roebuck might wish to buy Goldman Sachs, or some other securities house, and distribute investment products through its retail outlets. Moving the mysterious and opulent world of finance into the storefront alongside garden tools seemed to Levy and Cy Lewis to be nothing short of heresy. But neither man was able, in the presence of the Sears chief executive, to express his dismay. As Sandy expatiated on the idea, his father looked at him and growled, "Christ, your mouth goes like a duck's behind." That ended the conversation.

Following the trip, Lewis returned to White Weld, but with little hope that the frictions there would lessen. Later in January, Lewis lit into a valuable client, who went to the management to complain about the rude treatment he had received.

Immediately afterward, Lewis was fired. He had been there just short of three years.

The Sunday afternoon after he was jettisoned, Lewis answered the doorbell at his home and saw Jim Robinson, who had driven out from New York to say that he was sorry it had all ended on such an unpleasant note and that he hoped he and Lewis could stay in touch. Lewis was struck by Robinson's thoughtfulness and remembered the visit for years.

Sandy Lewis' next stop on Wall Street lasted less than a year. He took a position with Model Roland, a small but innovative trading house that had succeeded with many of the financial institutions during the late sixties. The firm soon altered its ownership structure along lines Lewis disagreed with, and he walked out. (Model Roland was later absorbed by Shields, forming Shields Model Roland, which was itself acquired by Bache.)

Wall Street was becoming a lonely place for Lewis. Although the securities industry offers an unusual level of camaraderie, financial people tend to distrust refugees from success. Many on Wall Street like the idea of cashing in on their friendships, but in those days Sandy Lewis seemed less and less a promising contact. His intelligence impressed people, yet his brash, volatile ways put them off. In addition, Lewis sometimes felt a need to be understood, so when his blunt talk or psychological analyses jarred people, he would insist on describing how Cy Lewis and Bruno Bettelheim shared his paternity. Such personal revelations were more than people wanted to hear. Lewis wasn't the only Wall Street financier with a troubled history, but he seemed to be one of the few who wanted to talk about it. Most others found it better to appear bullish.

Cy Lewis was alarmed that, for all his brilliance and promise, his eldest son seemed unable to adapt to life on Wall

Street. After the Model Roland job ended abruptly, the elder Lewis came home and broke into sobs. "Christ, I wonder if that boy will ever make a nickel," he said to Diana.

Still, jobs seemed to open up for Sandy as quickly as they ended. Not long after the Model Roland fiasco, Lewis began a series of negotiations with Dean Witter to help mount a major push into institutional trading. The firm was interested. Despite the bumpy career he'd led on Wall Street, Sandy Lewis was becoming well known in trading rooms. Fearful of giving away plans about the expansion of the trading operation, Dean Witter's management decided to keep the negotiations with Lewis top secret. One official devised a code name for Lewis: White Eagle. In April 1971, Lewis began working at the firm.

In the months that followed, Lewis helped to expand the trading operation substantially. He also had his first contact with the staff of the Securities and Exchange Commission in Washington, which sought his advice on setting up a reporting system whereby all trades in listed stocks would be disclosed instantaneously on electronic displays. More than other Wall Street executives, Lewis tended to be open with the regulators in Washington, often going out of his way to point out some practice he found to be unethical and urging them to outlaw it.

Lewis also decided to run for the local school board in his New Jersey town and took several weeks off in 1971 to visit classrooms and call on other parents to discuss the changes he wanted to see made in the Short Hills schools. In the end, Sandy lost the election, but he learned a lot about the schools his children attended.

In the following year there were some shifts at Dean Witter that left Lewis less secure in his position. One departure was that of Harry Nelson, with whom Lewis had worked at Salomon. Nelson played an important role in the trading operation and served as a buffer between Lewis and the Dean Witter managers he tended to antagonize. After he left, tensions between Lewis and his superiors mounted. "They came after me with knives," Lewis said years later.

The situation finally exploded over the failed political campaign of George McGovern. Lewis detested Richard Nixon, and though he thought McGovern had little chance of unseating him, he joined several prominent Wall Street Democrats in advising McGovern. Lewis' name subsequently appeared with the others' on the letterhead of a mailing sent to Wall Street executives by the McGovern campaign. This McGovern link sparked a nasty confrontation between Lewis and Robert Swinarton, a vice president of the staunchly Republican Dean Witter. Lewis' outburst took the form of an eloquent defense of civil liberties, but it nevertheless ended with the familiar result: Lewis was fired. The day of the White Eagle had ended.

Now Lewis balanced the vicissitudes and repeated failures of his life on Wall Street with the success and satisfaction in his home life. Having survived the wrenching effects of living with a family that was irrevocably unhappy, he was determined to foster a different kind of household. There were five children in the Lewis family by this time: Joshua, Jordan, Kari, John Benjamin, and Jeremy.

Whereas Cy Lewis' Wall Street prowess expanded and flourished, Sandy's career was battered and dented. But where Cy Lewis' family life had darkened into a miserably complicated tangle of resentments and disappointments, Sandy's was successful and robust. If Cy Lewis found the financial success his father had missed, Sandy created the family life Cy had never experienced. Each generation of Lewises tried to succeed where the preceding generation had failed.

After Lewis left Dean Witter, his family grew larger still. Barbara had a sixth child, a boy whom they named Oliver.

In addition, the Lewises adopted Valerie Ford, a neighbor and friend of the family whose parents had recently died. Val and her four siblings had lived for a time with foster parents, but the experience was unhappy. When she came to the Lewises', at fifteen, she was depressed, overweight, and more than a year behind in schooling because she had taken care of her younger siblings during the months of her mother's terminal illness. In other situations as well, Lewis continually sought opportunities to help young people. It was a way of expressing gratitude for his own rehabilitation.

But Lewis also needed to prove that he could succeed on Wall Street. After the debacle at Dean Witter, he learned about an expansion of the trading effort at Merrill Lynch, the largest brokerage house in the business, and decided to explore it. Merrill Lynch was not just bigger than other Wall Street firms; it was different. It was more like a modern American corporation than the many archaic companies on Wall Street. Lewis, naturally, was anything but a compliant organization man, but he thought that Merrill Lynch might be a more rational, efficient environment than many other financial houses.

A series of interviews with top Merrill Lynch executives went well. But Lewis' history in the business was worrisome to them. For his part, Lewis didn't want this job to end with another explosion of tempers in the trading room.

Cy Lewis, as he had repeatedly before, got directly involved. He set up a meeting with Donald T. Regan, the Merrill Lynch head and later President Reagan's chief of staff, at which he explained his son's troubled childhood, his treatment under Bruno Bettelheim, and his brash ways as an adult. Regan somehow liked the sound of the younger Lewis and decided in late 1972 to take him in.

6

With the completion of the Hayden Stone deal, a thinly capitalized and little-known securities house was able to count itself among Wall Street's major contenders. CBWL, which had five thousand accounts, suddenly found itself with fifty thousand; and after managing two offices, in New York and Beverly Hills, it had taken on another twenty-eight across the United States.

But the deal did something more. It provided the blueprint for a decade of acquisitions by Weill and his colleagues. Industry conditions played into their hands. By the 1970s, when things had turned sour for Wall Street, stocks no longer carried the promise of effortlessly achieved riches. Scores of investors had lost fortunes in the plunge of 1969 and the wilted markets of the ensuing years. Worse, many investors had been dismally served by their brokers, who had tangled up or lost their assets during the paperwork mess. Between 1970 and 1975, the shareholder population dwindled from 30.8 million to 25.2 million. And with the investors went the commissions that had nourished Wall Street during the 1960s.

The financial arena was strewn with the carcasses of dozens of old and once powerful firms. But their demise provided other financial houses with opportunities for growth. More than any single firm, Weill's emerged from the troubled decade a victor. Weill was continually stalking new takeover prospects. He would listen for the death rattle of one old firm after another. When he moved in for another takeover, Weill left never a moment's doubt about which firm was negotiating from strength and which from desperation.

Following the Hayden Stone deal, Sandy and Joan Weill bought an apartment at Seventy-ninth Street and Madison Avenue, within walking distance of Sandy's offices in the General Motors Building. There would be many nights spent mostly at the office, and weekends devoted entirely to the growth of his brokerage empire. Family trips would be rarities. An evening out meant having dinner with people who were somehow involved in the business.

Industry conditions kept Weill absorbed. The Wall Street failures and forced marriages were bound to occur — because of the lack of management talent, because of the inherently flimsy capital structures at many of the private firms, and because of the heavy reliance on economically unnatural sources of income, in particular the revenue derived from a cartel-like pricing system. Right and left, firms like Shearson Hamill, Kuhn Loeb, and Faulkner, Dawkins & Sullivan were collapsing under the weight of all this; Weill merely offered them the chance to make graceful exits.

Just to make matters more complicated, the decade of the 1970s opened with another important Wall Street development: securities firms were able to issue their own shares to the public. The issuance of shares, this most basic function of capitalism, had been denied to the bulk of the securities industry by New York Stock Exchange regulations stipulating that member firms be privately owned. The folly of insulating Wall Street from the benefits of capitalism was becoming clear during the crisis years of the late sixties and early seventies. Firms built on flimsy assets were collapsing like houses of cards, as was clearly demonstrated by the fall of Hayden Stone. Moreover, Wall Street was aging. Partners were retiring in droves and were pulling out their money. Shut off from the public securities markets, the firms lacked the means of readily replenishing their funds.

Merrill Lynch's president, Donald Regan — a driving force behind the modernization of the securities business — openly deplored the hidebound tendencies of the Street and called for rules changes to enable Big Board members to go public. Chiding his peers for their myopia, he began urging Wall Street to "try capitalism." He let it be known that Merrill Lynch would be one of the first to issue securities to the public. In his 1972 book *A View from the Street,* Regan wrote:

> A great paradox about Wall Street is that although its experts are the best in the world when it comes to analyzing the capital structure of the corporations they are looking at, and although its sermons to the outside world never fail to include some homilies about the conservative management of capital, the Street in general has managed its own capital poorly. For a long time, it was improvident as regards its future, and without fully realizing it, it took up some anti-capitalistic postures.

Regan knew well what problems the partnerships encountered. Merrill Lynch itself functioned as a sprawling and unwieldy partnership until 1959, when it transformed itself into a private corporation. At one point, the vast brokerage house had 117 partners, each of whom signed a yearly agreement that set out his contractual obligations to the company. When additional cash was needed to finance the firm's aggressive expansion across the country, Charles Merrill, who fathered the huge brokerage company, would circulate among the partners, soliciting additional capital from each of them.

As more securities firms found themselves in severe financial straits and protests began to swell, the Exchange responded in a plodding, bureaucratic, and, many felt, dilatory fashion. The Big Board created what seemed like an endless number of committees; they studied the issue, drew up reports, and, as a rule, shelved the reports for further discussion. There was a deep, tribal resistance to changes that would put Wall Street on comparable footing with other segments of American commerce. The old guard was protecting a way of life.

The changes, of course, would be ushered in by Wall Street's mavericks and outlanders.

In 1969, Dan Lufkin, the thirty-seven-year-old chief executive of Donaldson, Lufkin & Jenrette, rose to the esteemed position of member of the New York Stock Exchange Board of Governors. The establishment had made way for the new generation. On May 21, 1969, in the palatial board room, surrounded by portraits of the early chiefs of the Exchange and sundry gifts of state from foreign entities, the youthful Lufkin announced that DLJ was in the process of filing a registration statement with the Securities and Exchange Commission for the purpose of issuing shares to the public. Since this was, of course, in open violation of the Exchange regulations, Lufkin explained that if the Exchange couldn't find its way clear to changing the rules, DLJ would simply

give up its membership, thereby freeing itself of the con-
straints imposed by the anachronistic regulations.

DLJ may have had reams of logic to support its radical
move, but it was assaulting the tenets of belief on Wall Street,
and the old guard immediately reacted with defensiveness.
There was as much objection to the style of Lufkin's declaration as to its substance. Bunny Lasker, the tireless Big Board
chairman, fairly roared with indignation. For a new governor
to announce that his firm was going public was, Lasker felt,
an act of unforgivable arrogance. The Exchange was, after
all, studying the question of allowing members to go public,
and the impatience of a new firm was viewed as disruptive
in the extreme. Lazard's Felix Rohatyn later wrote to Lufkin,
characterizing him as Judas Iscariot for his action at the board
meeting.

As the DLJ men saw it, however, the Exchange would
have tabled proposals to allow public ownership indefinitely
if there hadn't been some catalyst. Besides, DLJ had economic
worries, and it wanted to raise $24 million in the market. In
1969, it figured it could do so without much trouble, but it
couldn't count indefinitely on its favorable image. Trouble
at Hayden Stone and several other firms was already apparent.
"Time was running out for the industry," said Dick Jenrette.
He, too, saw the handwriting on the wall, and he believed
that the institutional brokerage lode of the 1960s was almost
used up. The pressure was building to allow institutions to
negotiate discounts off the Exchange rates. And there had
been signals from the Department of Justice that there might
be antitrust problems associated with excluding the investing
institutions from Exchange membership. With these clouds
on the horizon, DLJ figured it was prudent to raise money
sooner rather than later.

The need for permanent capital on Wall Street was breath-
takingly obvious, but there seemed to be strong sentiment

against public ownership. There was, simply, an innate disposition toward privacy. Publicly held companies, as any corporate finance specialist well knew, operated in a fishbowl. They were required to reveal their problems and shortcomings, since shareholders had a right to know about such things. On Wall Street, by contrast, a poor performance could be dealt with discreetly at a partners' lunch. Bonuses might be pared that year, perhaps, or a few back-office workers furloughed. The public needn't be told of the problem, unless it jeopardized a firm's survival, and partners needn't be pestered by reporters, telephoning to learn each detail of their ill fortune.

But the resistance to DLJ's move was based on more than an industry fetish for privacy. Access to the public capital markets would open the way for the new breed on Wall Street to assume positions that had considerable clout. The old private firms had spent most of the century building up their capital. It disturbed officers at these houses to realize that others could rake in comparable amounts simply by filing prospectuses with the SEC and issuing shares to the public.

There was also the question of just who would own stock in the securities houses. If shares were freely available, what would prevent companies that were outside the financial enclave from buying in? Most feared were the financial institutions themselves, in particular the banks. Already, the institutions had come to dominate the stock markets, and there was the fear that they would also move to seize control over the intermediaries operating within those markets.

On the other hand, there were personal economic factors that supported the notion of public ownership. Many Wall Street professionals had most of their assets tied up in the firms where they worked. When they retired, they cashed in by selling their stakes at book value. Public ownership would create a broadened marketplace for the stock of the securities houses, and it could give Wall Street professionals a better return on their holdings. Rather than selling out at book value, they would be able to get whatever multiple of book value the marketplace was paying.

But with a Big Board rule change made in April 1970, public ownership won the day. Capitalism had arrived on Wall Street. Power was seeping away from the Exchange toward the stronger firms in the business. Sensitive to the trend, the Big Board stated, in issuing the new rules, that despite the possibility of public ownership, there would be "meaningful self-regulatory control by the Exchange." For example, anyone seeking to hold more than half the voting stock in a member firm would be required to obtain the approval of the Exchange.

On April 9, 1970, DLJ sold 800,000 shares at $15 apiece, a substantially lower price than the firm had originally planned. But the stock market was mired in gloom, and Wall Street was beset by woes. Even the $15 price wasn't sustained; later that year, DLJ shares were trading at around $5 apiece. Nonetheless, DLJ had opened the way for other firms to offer their shares to the public.

CBWL–Hayden Stone filed a registration statement with the SEC on June 28, 1971. The firm planned to sell a million shares to the public at a maximum price of $17 a share. The offering would not only secure a solid capital base to support the company's future expansion; it would make instant millionaires of the partners, who had substantial chunks of stock in the firm. The summer of 1971 brought a brisk rally in the stock market that, along with the promotional efforts of the partners, positioned the firm for a successful offering.

But these weren't days when anything could be considered much of a sure thing. The SEC had suddenly declared that it would view with disfavor insiders at firms cashing in their own shares when a company went public. Part of CBWL's plan was that Cogan, Weill, Levitt, and Berlind would sell their shares. Each had spent most of the decade building up stock in the firm as his major investment. They were ready to consolidate the gains. Ken Bialkin went to Washington the Friday preceding the offering to meet with the SEC. There were only two commissioners in town that day, and three were needed for a vote. SEC Chairman William Casey (later to become the CIA chief in the Reagan administration) was in New York that day to meet with officials at the Stock Exchange. Levitt and Weill tracked him down, jammed into a taxi with him, and argued the merits of the stock sale all the way to Bethpage, Long Island, where Casey was due for a meeting. When the SEC chairman finally tumbled out of the taxi in Bethpage, Weill turned to the cab driver. "Would you go along with us if you were in his spot?" he asked. The driver, somewhat shell-shocked, replied, "I wouldn't know how *not* to." Then he added, "You guys are some kind of crazy." His fare came to $68.

Casey's response was in sync with the cab driver's, it turned out. The partners would be allowed to sell their own shares during the offering. Then another problem cropped up. While partners were out pitching the firm's stock to their customers, they had to contend with a Cassandra in their midst. David Bostian, an influential analyst employed by CBWL–Hayden Stone, was being overly pessimistic about the market. Bostian had an M.B.A. from the University of North Carolina and was one of the masters of technical analysis, a highly mathematical approach to market research. One of his devices was a gauge he called the "intraday intensity index." If the stocks closed at either the intraday high on increased trading volume or at the intraday low on descending volume, Bostian was bullish. The reverse positions produced a bearish reading. By September, the summer rally had ended, and Bostian's intraday signals were gloomy. Moreover, the analyst began getting considerable publicity in the *Wall Street Journal* and the financial columns by saying so. Attention from the press was usually welcome, but it wasn't at the time when CBWL–Hayden Stone was readying its own stock offering. How could Levitt and Cogan and Berlind and Weill tell their customers to buy CBWL stock when their own technical analyst was saying stocks in general were about to plunge? The partners were advised by their attorneys that they should withdraw a printed prospectus for the offering and turn out a new one that included at least some mention of Bostian's dismal prognosis for the stock market. This they did, and Bostian came under the scorching glare of the firm's principals, who were seething about the entire development.

Things took a turn for the worse on the morning of October 4, 1971, the day of the offering. That morning, the *Wall Street Journal* market columnist Dan Dorfman wrote the following:

It's anybody's guess how the shares of CBWL–Hayden Stone will fare when they probably begin trading today. But if you buy the view of its director of technical market studies, David Bostian, the near-term outlook for this stock, or any stock for that matter, is pretty poor. Mr. Bostian, who had called bullish moves in the market three times in the past year, early last month predicted a sharp decline in the Dow Jones industrial average to about the 790 or 800 level by year-end. And he forecast an even deeper drop to about 750 if any government controls on corporate profits develop. It isn't any secret that Mr. Bostian currently is as bearish as ever, with a suggested cash position of at least 50%. Under the category of "risk factors" in the prospectus, there isn't any reference to Mr. Bostian's gloomy outlook. However, buried deep in the report on page 24 under the heading "research services" is a reference to an employee who predicted "substantial declines" in market averages.

The partners nervously tried to assure one another that everything would turn out all right. Marshall Cogan had devoted hours to persuading traders throughout the business to buy shares in CBWL–Hayden Stone when they were offered. Investors were told that the market had its ups and downs and that the brokerage firms had more than their share of volatile earnings as well. But investors had seen the dizzying heights of Wall Street's profits during the sixties. Good times would return, and buying shares in a securities firm was one way to cash in on that prospect. As it happened, the CBWL–Hayden Stone offering turned out to be a sellout. The shares were snapped up at $12.50 apiece on the first day, and because of additional buying interest, prices for the stock rose to about $13 later that day. Existing shareholders, who numbered twenty-five, liquidated a sheaf of stock before the offering and also sold 400,000 shares to investors in the course of the transaction. Weill, the kid from Brooklyn, had become a millionaire, as had each of the other principal partners.

It was another victory. The firm had acquired, through the Hayden Stone deal, the prestige of Wall Street history, and now it had shored up a permanent capital base through its initial public offering of stock. But it was part of an industry beset by changing rules, sluggish markets, and a steady exodus of customers. The year of 1972 was bleak. Underwriting business slackened off, and brokerage commissions were drying up. For its fourth quarter, ending June 30, earnings had plunged from a year earlier. Then, for the quarter ending September 30, the company did no more than break even. On September 29, Berlind explained at the company's first annual shareholders' meeting that "volume levels are pitifully low, and at today's level of activity, our company is essentially a break-even activity." The problems weren't unique to CBWL–Hayden Stone. Firms that had invested in computers and personnel to handle steadily growing volume now found themselves on the ropes. In 1972, an average day on the Big Board saw a puny sixteen million shares change hands. In the third week in September, two smaller securities firms,

Rifkind & Company and Butler Capital Corporation, were pushed out of the business. Other failures loomed.

On October 25, Marshall Cogan presented his firm's board of directors with a memorandum detailing the existential gloom that he felt pervaded the place. The memo stated: "The firm is progressing toward a mediocre and banal existence — that euphoric involvement we were once able to generate is getting harder to create. I am terrified at our present inability to function as an integrated entity. The lack of commitment to the firm is appalling." He stated that "the deterioration of revenue particularly at the branch level has reached serious proportions." He characterized as "chaotic" the company's methods of distributing information to its network of offices. He also lashed out at the way the company trained its new brokers. Like most of its competitors on Wall Street, the firm put little money into training stockbrokers. Merrill Lynch offered a comprehensive training program, as did Bache, but Hayden Stone and most others tended to pirate trained brokers from these firms.

The memorandum revealed a great deal about Marshall Cogan's own state of mind. Institutional brokerage was the chariot he had ridden through the sixties, and the race was drawing to a close. He ended the memo with the statement "Cogan, Berlind, Weill & Levitt is dead; [its] flexibility is dead."

Part of the problem, Cogan felt, was the lack of clear leadership. The company was far too large to continue operating under its original four-man leadership. Some one person would have to take the reins if it was to succeed as a major retail-oriented securities firm. In his memo, Cogan called for a leader who was "an extrovert an a driver," quoting words used by David Rockefeller during a recent management shakeout at the Chase Manhattan Bank. Cogan was such a man, and so was Weill. Berlind wasn't, and Levitt had essentially conceded the chief executive role to the others in 1969. At first, Weill hung back from taking charge of the firm; he felt more comfortable in the role of second-guesser.

But as the months wore on, the contest for directing the firm's future was between Cogan and Weill. It wasn't simply a matter of which man would run the company; it was also a matter of what the company would be. Cogan, who felt that the conventional brokerage business was suffering a malaise, was inclined to shrink the firm and to create a new mission for it as a merchant bank, which would make money by buying and selling companies and helping corporations structure unusual deals and transactions. Weill, however, was committed to the steady expansion of the company in the retail brokerage trade. He had overseen the construction of an efficient back-office system, and he believed it would pay off only if there was more and more business. The analogy that gained currency around the firm was that Weill had built a giant salami slicer; it was now the firm's obligation to bring in more salami to be sliced.

It became clear that Weill was going to win the competition for the control of the company. Levitt, functioning as a swing vote, as he had four years earlier during the confrontation over Carter's role, sided with Weill. Although he was closer to Cogan personally, he felt that his friend was too brash, too rough-edged, to run a major, publicly owned corporation. Levitt, ever conscious of the image he and his partners projected, believed that Weill, Brooklyn background notwithstanding, would present a more polished façade — or that he could learn to. The partners were determined to trade up, to remake their image. As part of this endeavor, they decided to drop CBWL and go by the older name, Hayden Stone. And they anointed Sandy Weill as leader of the firm. Cogan, defeated, left the company and, as it turned out, the brokerage business.

* * *

In some respects, the new title of chief executive and chairman changed Weill. He strove to fit the role of a Wall Street chieftain. In the 1960s, an associate scoffed, "Weill could be an embarrassment; his teeth were yellow and he always had gravy on his tie; his clients were the butcher, the baker, and the candlestick-maker from Brooklyn." Now Weill was in command. Rather than neglecting his modest beginnings, he used them to dramatize his ascent and the impressive growth of his firm. Milton Fenster, a long-time friend of Paul Mosher, Joan Weill's father, served as the firm's public relations counsel and helped drum up a flurry of press reports over the years, most of which played up the theme the Brooklyn boy turned millionaire.

Weill's insecurities, however, didn't disappear. Nor was the task of establishing his firm among the older and more respected financial houses of Wall Street a simple one. In 1973, the year Weill took the helm, events seemed to trip him up, as they had when he was younger. That year, both the firm and Weill himself faced an enforcement action by the Securities and Exchange Commission over an underwriting Weill had arranged in 1971 for a toy manufacturer, Topper Corporation. Weill, a board member of the company, had set up the deal whereby Topper offered to the public $5.25 million in debentures.

The federal agency felt that, as underwriter, Weill and his firm knew the projections were inflated and either joined the client in misleading investors, or were negligent in not noticing that Topper was issuing fraudulent information about itself. In November 1973, the agency charged both Topper and Hayden Stone with fraud. The securities firm emphatically denied wrongdoing, insisting that Topper had, in fact, intentionally defrauded Hayden Stone, along with its own auditors and lawyers. But the American Stock Exchange also took action, fining Hayden Stone $20,000 for failing to make an "independent inquiry" into Topper's true condition.

Shortly before Cogan left, he helped the firm make another crucial move in its expansion-by-acquisition strategy. This was the April 1973 merger with H. Hentz & Company, which almost doubled the size of the company. Hentz was a prestigious Wall Street name, with a strong commodities business, a string of offices in Europe — and very many financial problems. What thrust it into the jaws of Hayden Stone was one of the most startling incidents of corporate corruption in the history of finance — the Equity Funding scandal.

Equity Funding, a West Coast insurance concern, entered bankruptcy earlier that year after it was revealed that the company had fabricated hundreds of insurance policies. Stanley Goldblum, former chairman of Equity Funding, went to jail for his part in the scam, but until the analyst Ray Dirks blew the whistle on the scheme, Equity Funding was a popular stock among institutional money managers. One of these hapless investors was a holding company called Fidelity Corporation of Virginia, which had agreed in early 1973 to rescue Hentz. Left with 579,000 virtually worthless shares of the scandal-ridden Equity Funding, Fidelity was forced to pull out at the eleventh hour. As they had done during the Hayden Stone crisis, Weill and his partners rushed in to fill the void.

There was something skewed about the manner in which Weill's firm merged with other companies, but as long as those companies were themselves in death throes, no one seemed to object. Simply put, Weill arranged to acquire companies with their own money. Usually an acquiring company has less capital after it buys another company. Weill's firm invariably had more capital after each acquisition. Subordinated lenders and partners in the moribund companies Weill bought were just as happy to move their money over to a firm that seemed to be at least viable, perhaps even successful. So with $7 million from Hayden Stone's lenders and $11 million from Hentz's, along with retained earnings and the proceeds of the public offering, Weill's firm had about $32 million in capital. Through the Hentz deal, it took on another twenty-nine domestic branches, seventeen of which were located in cities where Hayden Stone had offices. Later in 1973, Weill's firm snapped up the small brokerage of Saul Lerner & Company.

The "failing firms strategy" was solidly in place when Wall Street dragged into the recession of 1973 and 1974. Dozens of firms were collapsing, and investors of all stripes were fleeing the scene. Institutions reversed their earlier rush into stocks and en masse loaded up on bonds. More Wall Street firms were being pushed to the brink meanwhile. In January 1974, Du Pont Walston, Inc., filed for Chapter 11 bankruptcy reorganization after shedding its business. By this time, fortunately, there were fewer worries that a Wall Street panic would result from one failure. Three months after the 1970 Hayden Stone debacle, Congress had enacted a bill that set up the Securities Investor Protection Corporation, which guarantees investor assets up to set levels if their brokerage firms go under. Kidder Peabody's Ralph De Nunzio, a stalwart member of the New York Stock Exchange's 1970 crisis committee, helped to draft the legislation and to get the new agency in place. It was funded by the securities firms, with a backup by the federal government, so that a string of failures would still cost the industry money. By the spring of 1974, other old firms were faltering. In May, Clark, Dodge & Company, a medium-size firm with a carriage-trade clientele, was pushed into a merger with Kidder Peabody. A week later, it was learned that the seventy-four-year-old Shearson, Hammill & Company, itself in tight financial straits, was talking merger with Hayden Stone.

Like other Weill acquisition targets, Shearson Hammill had been jilted by another suitor, Carl Lindner of the American

Financial Group. The merger that now resulted brought about another name change — Shearson Hayden Stone. With each change, Weill tried to acquire more of the prestige that his firm conspicuously lacked; each merger brought a new connection with Wall Street's past. Weill and his partners were trying to buy prestige.

With the Shearson Hammill merger, Weill became ruthlessly efficient at deciding who would survive at the newly formed company. By Labor Day of 1974 — two weeks before the combination was even complete — Weill had cut off nearly twelve hundred employees, mostly Shearson Hammill's. Weill was both criticized and praised for his ability with the scalpel. Admirers said he made mergers succeed by deciding immediately which people to keep; the jobless learned of their status quickly, which Weill argued was better for them. Critics said Weill was merciless in laying off employees during merger proceedings. Indeed, given the unequaled succession of mergers effected by Sandy Weill, it is safe to say that more of the financial executives around Wall Street who were fired were laid off by Sandy Weill than by any other person in the business. Some, but by no means all, were bitter about it. Many simply recognized the law of the Wall Street jungle. A few seemed to relish the great Darwinian drama Weill was playing out, even when it operated to their immediate disadvantage. One talented analyst shed by Weill late in the seventies later praised his ability to discard employees by the truckload.

In 1975, despite intensive lobbying by Wall Street's old guard, Congress enacted the Securities Acts Amendments, which, as we have seen, directed the Securities and Exchange Commission to abolish the treasured fixed commissions. The federal agency accomplished this on May 1, since known in the business as May Day.

The pressures brought by competitive commissions seemed

to play into Sandy Weill's hands. Shearson Hayden Stone snapped up Chicago-based Lamson Brothers in 1976 and a year later bought one of its early rivals in the institutional brokerage trade, Faulkner, Dawkins & Sullivan, and brought Dwight Faulkner into the top echelon of the growing securities company.

The old partnership by this time had split completely. In 1975, two years after Cogan's departure, Roger Berlind left, following a devastating personal tragedy. On June 24, 1975, Berlind's wife and three of his four children were killed in a plane crash. His youngest, William Berlind, then two years old, had remained at home. Berlind resigned a week later. "I wasn't in any shape to do anything useful at the firm," he said, "and I didn't want to be there." Berlind spent a year mostly at home, taking care of his son and absorbing the impact of the tragedy. When he emerged from this transitional period, it was to return to his first love, the theater. He became a successful producer and eventually brought out several successes, including *Sophisticated Ladies, Amadeus, Nine,* and *The Real Thing.*

Arthur Levitt remained the president of Shearson Hayden Stone until 1977, when, weary of answering to the strong-willed Sandy Weill, he left to become chairman of the American Stock Exchange.

Weill, in the meanwhile, had created a force behind the throne in a whiz-kid former analyst, Peter Cohen. Originally brought in by Cogan, the twenty-six-year-old Cohen became Weill's aide-de-camp in 1973, right after his first boss's departure. Small, intense, and mathematical, Cohen scrutinized the details of each deal and masterminded the complicated procedures needed to meld two companies without creating accounting confusions. He took care of the machinery involved in building a brokerage empire without threatening Weill's hegemony.

In early November 1977, Weill set out to buy prestige once again, this time in the old-line investment bank of Kuhn Loeb. Weill, always concerned about his firm's image, wanted to acquire Kuhn Loeb's century-old reputation and its hefty list of corporate finance clients. Shearson's international business would have expanded substantially with the addition of Kuhn Loeb's global financiers. The Shearson Hayden Stone men met with Harvey Krueger, a top Kuhn Loeb executive, and a small group of his advisers one Friday at the offices of Willkie, Farr & Gallagher. The deal seemed to be in place, and Weill was ebullient over his latest catch.

Weill and his men arrived for the final meeting, but the Kuhn Loeb team did not. Shearson, in the words of one top executive there, was "the jilted bridegroom." The wealthy Schiff family, which owned a sizable chunk of Kuhn Loeb and had long called the shots at the firm, viewed a merger with Shearson Hayden Stone as a clash of cultures. Weill's company lacked prominent corporate clients. Its executives moved in different circles from those of "our crowd" financiers at Kuhn Loeb, who quickly put together a more compatible merger with Lehman Brothers.

Kuhn Loeb's move to Lehman, and the cavalier manner in which it was made, was a snub to Shearson Hayden Stone. "It was a terrible blow to Sandy's ego," an associate said later. But in 1979 Weill was back on the acquisition trail, picking up part of Reinholt & Gardner, a regional firm, and Western Pacific Financial Corporation, a mortgage banker.

Next came the merger with Loeb Rhoades Hornblower, which was presided over by the venerable John Loeb and was much larger than Kuhn Loeb. Loeb Rhoades had bought Hornblower Weeks, Noyes & Trask in January 1978, forming Loeb Rhoades Hornblower. But the merger hadn't worked. The combination of the two companies' operational systems had been poorly managed, resulting in endless foul-ups in processing customer orders and recording transactions.

The two companies had set up a troika to run the company, but the arrangement was both unpleasant and inefficient. The three — Thomas Kempner, John Toolan, and Sherman Lewis — seemed to move on separate tracks and often disagreed or simply failed to communicate with one another. Behind the troubled company was John Loeb, who had built the firm up from its formation in 1931 and who in 1979 viewed his firm's financial condition with increasing consternation.

In the spring of 1979, some talks between Weill and Kempner, John Loeb's nephew, made a merger with Shearson seem a likely prospect. As in past mergers, Weill's company was buying a firm larger than it was. Loeb Rhoades had about 150 domestic offices, compared with Shearson's 130. Brokers numbered eighteen hundred at Loeb Rhoades, compared with seventeen hundred at Shearson. Most important, Weill was once again acquiring part of Wall Street's establishment cachet. John Loeb, then seventy-six, had rebuffed Weill and his partners ten years earlier, when they had come to him to plead that Loeb Rhoades accept their little-known firm, Cogan, Berlind, Weill & Levitt, as a correspondent broker.

The merger plan was negotiated on the May 12–13 weekend at the estate Weill had bought in Greenwich. Executives from the various offices of the two companies were flown in throughout the weekend. John Loeb, though not present, was in touch by telephone and was kept apprised throughout the weekend. The merger, which was announced on Monday, May 14, symbolized, more than any that had preceded it, the yielding of the old Wall Street power. The deal was a blow to John Loeb's pride; he insisted that the press release describe it as a "combination." But no one saw it as anything but a takeover, Weill's crowning acquisition. The new firm was named Shearson Loeb Rhoades and would have just over $250 million in capital, second in size to Merrill Lynch. Shearson Loeb Rhoades contained remnants of at least twelve formerly independent securities companies. Just on the Shearson side alone, there was Hayden Stone, Shearson Hammill, Hentz, Lamson Brothers, Faulkner Dawkins, Saul Lerner, and Rheinholdt & Gardner. The Loeb side brought remainders of Hornblower Weeks, Hemphill Noyes, Spencer Trask, and, of course, Carl M. Loeb and Rhoades & Company.

Over the summer and fall, Shearson consolidated the two firms' operations in research, block trading, domestic customer sales, bonds, and marketing. By the start of 1980, the Loeb operation was fully absorbed by Shearson, and Weill's much-enlarged firm was poised for what was to become an unprecedented period of profits for Wall Street. Nineteen eighty was aptly described by *Institutional Investor,* Wall Street's major trade magazine, as "the year it rained money." It was a time when everything seemed to be working toward prosperity for the securities houses. Large pension funds had watched allegedly conservative bond holdings shrivel in value because of surging interest rates, which undercut the market value of older, lower-yielding bonds. Such shrunken bond portfolios drove institutional investors into stocks. And because the equity markets themselves were volatile, the big institutional investors were forced to move as nimbly as possible. More than ever, money was in flux, and movement was good for Wall Street.

In 1970, an average trading day on the New York Stock Exchange saw 11.5 million shares change hands, with an annual turnover rate of 19 percent. In 1980, an average day on the Big Board saw a volume of 44.8 million shares, with a turnover rate of 36 percent. Peak trading days soared to levels Wall Street hadn't dreamed were possible. On November 5, the day following Ronald Reagan's landslide election, an exuberant burst of capitalist enthusiasm sent trading volume to 84.3 million shares.

High interest rates themselves, an albatross for many other sectors, were a boon to firms like Shearson. The money rig assembled in the 1970s brought forth a gusher when rates climbed above 15 percent. Brokers were in the consumer credit business, extending margin, or credit, to customers to buy securities. On a large scale, this was hugely profitable under high rates.

During the twelve months ending June 30, 1980, Shearson chalked up profits of $55.8 million — following taxes and a $10 million profits' distribution to the Loebs. That compared with $20 million the previous year and $10 million in 1978. Commissions zoomed to $327 million, from $189 million in 1979. And net interest income — from the customer credit business — came to $71 million. Overall, Shearson had the highest profit margins of any publicly traded securities firm. With the new success, the firm began to display more of the trappings of prestige. In 1979, with the help of Milton Fenster, the public relations man, Shearson lured former President Gerald Ford to serve as a board director and paid consultant.

Weill had moved the firm's headquarters to a palatial suite on the 106th floor of one of the World Trade Center towers; he himself had staked out a vast corner office that enjoyed a spectacular view of Manhattan stretching north on one side and the Verrazano-Narrows Bridge and Brooklyn on the other. The focal point of the office was a huge working fireplace; it was one of the early requests the Shearson chief executive had made when discussing a move to the World Trade Center. Considerable effort was expended to make sure it actually worked, including consultations with an aged fireplace expert about improving the draft. Between the many windows in the office was smooth pine paneling. Weill's desk was an antique, semicircular "hunt" desk. The headquarters held sumptuous reception rooms, a huge kitchen, and an elegant dining room with a mural. The artist had painted in many Wall Street fixtures and symbols, as well as countless references to Shearson and its booming success. Prominent in the mural was a depiction of Sandy Weill shaking hands with Gerald Ford; the image seemed an icon to the arduous climb Weill had begun twenty years earlier.

7

While Sandy Weill's firm was striving to become the second largest house on Wall Street, Merrill Lynch, the largest, was breaking new ground of its own. Assured of being the biggest broker for the time being, its energies went into reforming aspects of the securities business and expanding into other businesses.

Merrill Lynch was always a few steps ahead of its Wall Street rivals when it came to innovation. It was the first firm in the 1940s to set up a nationwide network of branch offices — part of Charles Merrill's program to "take Wall Street to Main Street." For many years it was the only firm to offer a comprehensive training program for securities brokers. It was the first firm to advertise on television and in the print media. It also incorporated the computer into its business before other big firms did.

Merrill Lynch simply operated under a different ethos. Though most Wall Street firms embraced entrepreneurial, freewheeling ways, and shunned conventional corporate management techniques, Merrill Lynch embraced them. Donald Regan ordered his working divisions to draw up five-year plans that set out their objectives, and he held them to those goals when compensation packages were considered. (At other Wall Street firms, according to a popular joke, planning consisted of scheduling the following day's lunch.)

Regan, tall, self-assured, and mettlesome, set the tone at Merrill Lynch. He enjoyed challenging the convention-ally held tenets of Wall Street. In *A View from the Street,* he even suggested that the securities industry wasn't just old-fashioned, but childishly sentimental:

> In every old man there lives something of a child. This is continuity and we have good reason to cherish it. But we do not expect an adult to suck his thumb all his life. The analogy is simple enough: we can keep part of the past with us. But we've got to dismiss what I can only describe as a fear of growing up.

When Sandy Lewis took a job at Merrill Lynch in 1972, some of his iconoclastic ways seemed compatible with Re-gan's. The Merrill Lynch chief had joined the firm in 1946 as a broker-in-training and had ascended to the presidency in April 1968. But Regan stood outside the clubby practices on Wall Street, preferring the independence he wielded at the gigantic Merrill Lynch. He didn't necessarily agree with Lewis on all issues — and their differences became more pro-nounced over time — but both were men who, for different reasons, did not accept the collective values in the securities business.

Deregulation of brokerage commissions had produced an acute decline in the sums brokers earned from institutional investors, but for Merrill Lynch it was a chance to snatch up the institutional brokerage business by slashing rates. Long identified with selling stock to individual investors, the firm began offering brokerage services to the banks, pension funds, and insurance companies at sharply discounted rates. Here, Merrill had the advantage of size: more thinly capitalized firms couldn't afford to match the rock-bottom prices it was offering. For their part, the investing institutions were obliged to seek the lowest available transaction costs, and, as a consequence, many of the smaller securities firms suffered. Several of the better-known institutional stock brokerage firms — such as Baker Weeks, Mitchell Hutchins, and Faulkner, Dawkins & Sullivan — decided to merge with larger securities firms rather than go it alone under this confluence of economic pressures. Donaldson, Lufkin & Jenrette, the premier institutional brokerage and research house of the 1960s, managed to hang on to its independence but saw its profits shrivel.

During the shakeout of institutional brokerage firms, Merrill Lynch was busy picking up securities analysts by furnishing salaries others weren't willing to pay in those meager times, or by offering them a safe harbor at a time when Wall Street houses were being merged out of existence almost weekly. One Wall Street executive called the recruitment effort at Merrill Lynch "a ruthless campaign by Regan." Perhaps it was. But Regan, like Sandy Weill, saw the surrounding turbulence as the appropriate condition for building his empire. And Regan had made it his goal to become the leading employer of research analysts counted as "All Stars" by *Institutional Investor*. The chairman met his goal: in 1977, *Institutional Investor* dubbed Merrill Lynch the industry leader in research, as measured by the number of All-Star analysts on the payroll. And analysts were central to attracting the patronage of the big investing institutions.

Because of his aggressive rate-slashing and hiring practices, Regan was viewed as something of a Wall Street bully. Some whispered that there should be a Justice Department investigation of Merrill Lynch to determine whether it was engaging in "predatory pricing," or slashing prices to uneconomically low levels in order to drive competitors out of business. The Antitrust Division of the Justice Department, did, in fact, watch the industry closely in the years following the unfixing of commissions, but it focused chiefly on determining why most large brokerage firms weren't discounting off the old fixed rates for individuals, not why they were discounting for the institutional players.

Sandy Lewis learned what he could from Donald Regan. At times, he looked to the Merrill Lynch chairman in much the way he had looked to Bruno Bettelheim in his Chicago years, as a mentor. "I rented his brain for a while," Lewis later said of Regan.

Sandy Lewis himself played several roles at Merrill Lynch between 1972 and 1977. He was a trader and arbitrageur, helping build up Merrill Lynch's strength, often drawing on the instincts, advice, and professional contacts of his father. He was a strategist, leaving the trading-pit atmosphere of his father and delving into the complex challenges of turning the brokerage house into a modern financial services corporation. And, finally, he was something of a reformer, advising decision-makers in Washington on how they should reshape things on Wall Street. In all these roles, Lewis was frenetic, brash, and at times unpredictable. He once smuggled a financial reporter into the Merrill Lynch trading room — bypassing the firm's intricate press relations machinery — by telling the other traders that the reporter was the son-in-law of Leonid Brezhnev, studying capitalism in New York at the behest of the Kremlin. He assumed — correctly, it turned out — that a story this outlandish would never be questioned.

The reform aspect of Lewis' tenure at Merrill Lynch was centered on an enormously complex puzzle known as the "national market system." The term refers to a revision of the market structure, pressed for in Washington, in which the maximum orders to buy and sell would be brought together in a single auction, with as many dealers as possible participating. Part of what the Congress and the SEC desired was an end to the dominant status of the NYSE. Lewis, whom Regan asked to chair a Merrill Lynch committee on the national market system, approached the exercise as both a philosopher and a missionary, believing himself amply equipped to understand the complexities of the issue and to decide what would be right for Wall Street.

In the early 1970s, and for more than a century before, the New York Stock Exchange functioned de facto as the national market system, capturing nearly 90 percent of the business, with the remainder flowing to the regional stock exchanges and to a handful of dealers that didn't belong to the Big Board and that made markets in listed stocks in their own trading rooms. Led by the feisty Weeden & Company, these dealers formed what was called the third market. The Exchange had begun to complain about the business conducted away from its trading arena, lashing into Weeden and the other so-called third-market-makers for breaking up the central auction on the Exchange floor. There was a point to the protests: Weeden & Company could trade with the big financial institutions and effectively by-pass orders left on the floor of the New York Stock Exchange. Much the same thing happened when brokers took trades to the regional exchange. However, it was difficult for the policymakers in Washington to justify putting the competing market-makers out of business or forcing them to join the Exchange and conduct their business there. After all, they represented a rare form of competition in a system that functioned as a virtual monopoly for the market-makers on the floor of the New York Stock Exchange.

The system of Exchange market-makers was another Wall Street peculiarity, considering that the Exchange sat at the heart of the free-enterprise system. Essentially, it rested on promised franchises, guaranteed monopolies, and hereditary privilege. The Exchange assigned lists of stocks to a group of firms called specialists. These were such companies as Creem & Creem, Adler Coleman, and Lasker, Stern & Stone — not household names. They generally didn't deal directly with the public; they dealt with traders and floor brokers. They worked at "posts" on the trading floor, which looked like islands in the maelstrom. Specialists governed the trading action in the stocks they were assigned. This meant that they set the opening prices in those stocks each morning and had the right to halt trading during the day if the buy or sell orders fell badly out of balance. The specialists also kept the limit order books. These were logs of orders brought to the floor by brokers on behalf of customers: limit orders directed the broker to buy or sell shares once a stock hit a particular price. Specialists maintained a list of limit orders for each price level in a stock and saw that those orders were executed whenever the stock hit the specified prices. This fairly simple clerical task was an important part of giving customers a fair shake in the market. The limit order books also created large amounts of revenue for the specialists, who earned commissions for executing the limit orders. Altogether, the specialist firms brought in between $60 million and $100 million a year on the limit order commissions.

The specialists were also expected to trade with their own capital in ways that stabilized market action. In other words, they were asked to buy when prices were declining and to sell when there was heavy buying demand. Thus, the specialists' trading activities tended to narrow swings in prices, thus keeping the market orderly. The specialists often pointed to their responsibilities as onerous, but traders away from the floor reasoned that, by and large, the specialists' trading responsibilities served to enrich them. After all, money is made when traders buy in a declining market and sell in a rising market.

Much of the national market debate centered on the extent to which the New York Stock Exchange specialists would be forced to abide competition from other market-makers. Exchange rule 394 (later changed to 390) required that brokers belonging to the Exchange send orders in listed stocks to the New York Exchange or some other certified stock exchange. (Virtually all the business, the Big Board could rest assured, would come to its floor.) Members of Congress and some SEC officials perceived this rule as blatantly anticompetitive, since it required business to flow to certain market-makers, thereby discouraging others from competing. On the other hand, rule 394 had the virtue of funneling the order flow to central locations, where a reasonable auction could take place.

The debate over the trading restrictions raised another question: if rule 394 were yanked and member firms could trade stocks where they wanted, Merrill Lynch, Dean Witter, and others would begin making markets in their own trading rooms. Given the vast number of orders these firms garnered from their worldwide offices, they would become mini-exchanges in themselves.

As Regan and his top staff studied the question, they became convinced that Merrill Lynch should be allowed to buy and sell stocks for its own customers without taking orders to the Exchange for execution. Lewis helped to flesh out some of the analysis. But after a time he began to question the wisdom and fairness of letting a firm as large as Merrill Lynch by-pass the Exchange and trade as a principal with its retail clients.

When Merrill Lynch acted as agent for a customer, its

charge was simply to seek the best price for the customer. But when it was acting as principal (trading with its own capital), it had its own interest to serve. In other words, if a Merrill Lynch customer was selling shares and Merrill Lynch itself was the buyer, the firm's natural tendency was to pay the lowest price possible for the shares — within the limits of the generally accepted market value for the stock. And if the customer wanted to buy securities and Merrill Lynch became the seller, the firm tended to sell the shares at the highest reasonable price.

Lewis became convinced that the exchange specialist system, for all its faults, was superior to the system Don Regan envisioned. Lewis believed that Merrill Lynch was seeking to become too powerful; furthermore, he saw it as his duty, for the good of the financial markets, to prevent the plans from materializing. The fact that Lewis was working for Merrill Lynch made all this difficult.

During what was already a difficult period, Sandy encountered a new crisis. In late 1974, he learned that a growth on his back was a melanoma, a malignant tumor symptomatic of a form of cancer that can be fatal within months if it isn't halted. Sandy's doctors removed the tumor and performed biopsies on tissue from his back and under his arm; they determined that the cancer had not traveled to these areas. The crisis seemed to have passed when, in the spring of 1975, Sandy discovered that he had cancer in the glands in his neck. This required another operation, in which part of the lymphatic system was excised from his neck. In addition to the surgery, Lewis underwent an intensive chemotherapy program.

Lewis' outward reaction to the disease was stoical. His work schedule was not interrupted. Two days after his neck surgery, he was in Don Regan's office with bandages around his head, explaining why he believed Merrill Lynch should not seek to take market-making away from the Big Board specialists.

In many respects, the cancer was a reminder to Sandy that things could, despite all his efforts to control them, go haywire. Since experiencing the carefully shaped environment of the Orthogenic School, he had strived to mold the influences on him and his family. He had maintained distance from his parents and had shut out people whose attitudes or behavior he found unacceptable. He avoided unpleasant compromises by breaking ties with firms he didn't approve of, knowing that his wealth allowed him to do so without serious economic consequences for him and the family. Now, he was confronted with the alarming discovery that the cells in his body were wreaking havoc inside him. It seemed illogical, arbitrary. Then he began to face the situation in the most deliberate way that he could. He researched both the disease and its treatment. He notified people — including Dr. Bettelheim — that he was being treated for cancer. And he kept working on theories for the national market system.

Lewis seemed emboldened by the experience of the disease; he was even more likely to speak his mind than before. Once, during this period, he stunned a roomful of Merrill Lynch executives by insulting a physically imposing and generally feared boss at the company. The man was quizzing the group on a variety of questions in the manner of a drill sergeant, and Lewis became irritated. Suddenly, he snapped, "Well, there's no substitute for brains."

Although Lewis recoiled from the "doomed messiah" role, he continued to resist Regan on Merrill Lynch's national market ambitions. Life at the firm became miserable as the conflict grew more intense.

A resolution came in 1977 as a result of the change in administration in Washington.

Roderick Hills, a Ford appointee and an old friend of both

Cy and Sandy Lewis, stepped down as chairman of the SEC. Sandy Lewis lobbied unsuccessfully for the installation of Peter Solomon, an old friend and partner at Lehman Brothers and a man with strong contacts in the Democratic party. But the Carter administration favored Harold Williams, formerly with Norton Simon and dean of the business school of the University of California at Los Angeles. Williams was not knowledgeable about the national market system, but he had opinions on several other issues, such as corporate governance and public representation on corporate boards. After his name first came up, he met Lewis at a luncheon in New York. When he was finally named SEC chairman, he asked Lewis to serve as a special advisor to him on the national market debate, which was approaching a critical juncture. Hearings were to take place in the summer of 1977 on whether the commission should force repeal of rule 390 and other off-Board restrictions.

His invitation was attractive to Lewis for two reasons: it provided an excuse for an exit from Merrill Lynch, and, more important, it opened the prospect of his influencing the fate of Merrill Lynch's and other firms' national market proposals.

When he arrived in the sweltering capital in July 1977, Lewis pored over government documents on the securities laws, beginning with William O. Douglas' papers written during the 1930s.

He discovered, to his alarm, that Williams seemed to have been won over by the reform-minded staff, which favored allowing firms like Merrill Lynch to compete directly with the exchange specialists. In his most headstrong fashion, Lewis told the chairman that he wouldn't work for him if he continued to adopt the positions espoused by the staff, and then he explained for hours on end the dangers of weakening the Exchange and expanding the power base of firms like Merrill Lynch. The SEC chairman, not well versed in the national market issues, was uncomfortable with the idea of doing anything that might later be viewed as pulling the plug on the stock exchange system. Nor was he comfortable with thwarting Sandy Lewis, whose intensity on the national market issue disarmed him.

In the end, Williams slowed the momentum toward a radical change in the market system — much to the frustration of Merrill Lynch. Officials close to the issue in both Washington and New York later credited Lewis with the behind-the-scenes activity that left the Big Board, and not Merrill Lynch, in control of the market system. Of course, the debate continued for years afterward, and the steady increase in trading volume eventually forced more automation on the Exchange, including some trading systems advanced by Regan.

Merrill Lynch continued to offer, in aggressive fashion, an array of services that were not normally considered Wall Street's business. "What we're trying to do," Regan once said, "is see how many financial services we can perform for people — legally and profitably." A former English major, Regan used words precisely. When he said he wanted to see how many services could be performed legally, he meant that he was willing to push the firm right up to the limits of the various financial statutes. His strategists worked closely with his lawyers in one attempt after another to determine whether annoying laws left over from the post-Crash years might get in the way.

In the spring of 1980, the effect of Regan's successful expansion during the 1970s was dramatized in the actions of a particular customer. The client was an American Everyman — a mobile, hard-working family man, pursuing business success within a big corporation, providing material comforts for his family. His aspirations were unremarkable, and he wasn't particularly interested in the stock market. The man was an employee of American Airlines and was being transferred from New York to Dallas as a result of the company's decision to relocate its headquarters. First, Merrill Lynch Realty Associates brokered the sale of the man's house on Long Island. Another arm of the realty group helped him find a new home in Dallas. He obtained a mortgage through a Texas lender whose funds had come, in part, through two Merrill Lynch mortgage insurers, AMIC Corporation, and Family Life Insurance Company. He took out an insurance policy on his mortgage through Family Life. Finally, he opened an account with Merrill Lynch, Pierce, Fenner & Smith and began putting spare money in the Merrill Lynch Ready Assets fund, the largest fund in the country.

This was what Regan had visualized all along. In 1979, when *Fortune* named Merrill Lynch one of ten "business triumphs of the seventies," the magazine stated that "convenience packaging is not the only thing Merrill Lynch learned during the financially treacherous seventies. It also learned how to wrap itself around its customers."

And Regan succeeded in making corporations, as well as individuals, customers of Merrill Lynch. Corporate treasurers had previously looked to prestigious investment banking names like Morgan Stanley or Goldman Sachs to give the stamp of approval to new offerings and to put together syndicates for distributing the securities. Investment banking was a world of tradition and continuity, one that Regan was determined to invade.

As it happened, the quickest route into the business was located in Merrill Lynch's headquarters building at One Liberty Plaza. It was Sandy Lewis' old employer, White Weld. What Merrill Lynch's people liked was that the firm enjoyed the reputation of being a "white shoe" investment bank. Established in 1895 as Moffatt & White, it had built up a particular strength in the handling of private placements, or securities offerings made to a select roster of large institutional investors. The firm also had established a strong reputation for serving the financial needs of the energy business. White Weld employed a covey of well-heeled investment bankers, smooth, articulate men capable of entering a corporate office and conveying the impression of cool assurance and sound financial judgment. Most important, however, was that the firm was feeling financial strains around 1977. Markets that year had been dismal. For the last half, White Weld had an operating loss of $4.3 million, compared with profits of $5.8 million in the same period the year before. Underwritings were sluggish. Government bond traders at the firm were chalking up huge losses. White Weld had another problem, one that made the red ink even more ominous. Like other private corporations on Wall Street, it lacked a permanent capital base. When partners left, they took their money with them. Paul Hallingby, the tall, affable banker who ran White Weld, saw it in philosophical terms. The firm had sufficient capital, he reasoned, but virtually all of it was "mortal capital."

In late March 1978, Hallingby got a phone call from Don Regan. The timing couldn't have been more propitious. Merrill Lynch was vast and highly capitalized with money Hallingby could certainly consider immortal. White Weld was a presence in the tight circle of investment bankers where Merrill Lynch remained a parvenu.

After the close of trading on Friday, April 14, Hallingby called key staff members into the White Weld board room. A deal had been struck, he told them. Merrill Lynch would pay $50 million in cash for White Weld, approximately the book value of its stock. Hallingby would become the vice chairman of Merrill Lynch, Pierce, Fenner & Smith. Regan moved to set up a distinct investing banking subdivision within the supermarket, one that would strive to duplicate the atmosphere of the major investment banks.

Next, the firm embarked on further diversification outside the traditional securities business. Real estate emerged as a clear opportunity. The Merrill Lynch planners tallied up the numbers and determined that real estate transactions created commissions of about $12 billion in a good year, more than three times the volume of brokerage fees generated on Wall Street. Real estate was also a method for Merrill Lynch to attract younger customers than it would if it offered only investment services. The average brokerage customer was about fifty, but people usually were interested in real estate before the age of thirty-five. In 1977, Merrill Lynch edged into real estate with the acquisition of a relocation company, which it rechristened Merrill Lynch Relocation. It helped companies move employees by buying and selling houses all over the country. The activity, though not enormously profitable in itself, was an effective means of acquainting Merrill Lynch with the major real estate markets throughout the United States. After a while, the Wall Street giant sized up which mom-and-pop real estate agencies were the significant forces in various communities, and it plunged into the second phase of its real estate venture.

This entailed the steady purchase of local real estate agencies. Merrill Lynch Relocation dealt in home sales necessitated by corporate moves. Regan wanted to get involved in all types of home sales. Under his acquisition plans, a local entity would retain its name, adding that of Merrill Lynch Realty Associates and picking up the familiar logo of the bull. The tactic was the mirror image of that employed in the 1940s by Charles Merrill when he set up branch offices all over the country and called it "bringing Wall Street to Main Street." Dakin Ferris, the shrewd Atlantan who headed Merrill Lynch's real estate efforts, said his goal was to "bring Main Street to Wall Street" — by absorbing it.

In 1975, Merrill Lynch began the planning effort that led

to the creation of the firm's wildly successful Cash Management Account, the most important single financial innovation of the era.

The top planning job at Merrill Lynch was delegated to Thomas Chrystie, a big outdoorsman who had worked in the company's investment banking division. Tom Chrystie, who was a neighbor and friend of Sandy Lewis', shared Regan's predilection for tearing down the historic barriers in the financial business. Each saw the the shift from traditional brokerage as a way to lessen the firm's dependence on the stock market, which could fluctuate unpredictably. Just before taking on the planning job, Chrystie had been in charge of a committee that was examining possible changes in the 1933 Glass-Steagall Act, which had kept commercial banks out of most forms of investment banking. The majority of Wall Street firms were fearful that the act would be repealed and that the big banks would invade the securities business. Banks were already making inroads: Chemical Bank was offering customers brokerage services in New York; Chase was reinvesting dividends for customers.

Chrystie reviewed the reams of papers and studies on Glass-Steagall and came to the conclusion that the committee should disband. Describing his reaction several years later, Chrystie tapped a small oval coffee table with his broad hand and said, gesturing toward his roomy office, "Our business was the size of this table, and the banking business was the size of the rest of this room. I asked myself, Why are we trying to defend this little island? We shouldn't have a committee like this. The natural direction is for us to go into the rest of the room." As Chrystie saw it, Merrill should explore banklike services but avoid taking on the legal identity of a bank, which would force it to observe many strict federal regulations.

Accomplishing that move brought Merrill Lynch into intimate association in 1976 with a group of consultants at Palo

Alto's SRI International, formerly the Stanford Research Institute. Among the SRI advisers was Andrew Kahr, an independent consultant who had been brought in for certain securities industry projects.

Kahr was a somewhat alien figure to the Merrill Lynch people. Merrill Lynch was a company whose top management was dominated by big, plain-talking Irishmen; Kahr was a small, delicate man in his thirties with large, luminous brown eyes and a quizzical expression. The son of an art historian and a physician, he was raised in New York and had a bachelor's degree from Harvard and a doctorate in mathematics from MIT. After teaching at the Harvard Business School for five years, he took a job as the chief financial officer of Ventron Corporation, a chemical concern based in Boston. The experience was disappointing, and Kahr left two years later to enter the consulting business. His role as a consultant's consultant was nothing short of bizarre to Chrystie, who had a suspicious attitude toward all consultants. For his part, Kahr had a way of referring to particular businesses or business leaders as "dumb" or even "hopeless."

At one meeting of the SRI team and Merrill Lynch, the discussion turned to ways in which customers might put idle funds into a money market fund or some other interest-bearing account. Chrystie immediately challenged the idea. Wall Street used the billions in cash that customers left in their accounts for short periods. By paying customers interest on their money, Chrystie contended, the firm would be throwing away its "ace in the hole."

Kahr had a different view of things. "It's not your ace in the hole," he declared coolly. "It's your Achilles' heel." At a time of ravaging inflation and high interest rates, he argued, people were less likely to sit back while a financial intermediary earned interest on their money.

Indeed, the financial consumer was becoming more sophisticated, and the money business involved more than investing for capital gains. Individuals wanted to keep up with inflation, and at that time regulated interest-bearing bank accounts, paying in the range of 5 percent interest, didn't help them. Billions of dollars in personal assets were, in fact, up for grabs and would drift to whichever institutions offered vehicles that provided safety, convenience, and a means of staying, at the least, even with inflation.

Kahr suggested that a credit card might be linked with an investment account at Merrill Lynch, but since a securities firm couldn't legally join a credit card association, Merrill Lynch would have to collaborate with a bank. Some officials at the meeting, more wary than Chrystie, said this would be virtually impossible, because Merrill Lynch would be edging toward a service that was competing with the banks.

However, in the spring of 1976, a Columbus, Ohio, bank, called Bank One, agreed to manage the card and checking facets of Merrill Lynch's Cash Management Account. Now, even to Chrystie, the idea looked promising. Customers could draw funds from the Cash Management Account with a check or Visa card. Idle money would be automatically swept into a money market fund that got the top interest rates. All activities would be summarized in a single monthly statement.

Some of the concepts in the CMA plan had earlier been broached by Lewis at Merrill Lynch when he suggested the use of the computer to shift funds between a variety of different investments. The CMA was the ultimate "packaged product" of finance.

Regan took the idea to the Merrill Lynch executive committee in 1976, and it responded with considerable enthusiasm. Afterward, Chrystie assembled the forty-odd Merrill Lynch employees who had for months given up their own time to work on the project. He wanted to thank them for the long hours they had volunteered and to map out an agenda for the company to follow in proceeding with the program. Before addressing the group, Chrystie met privately with Regan. Both agreed that the project was well on its way and that it represented a revolutionary concept in financial services. Then Regan stated that absolutely no one in the company, outside the executive committee, was to know about the program. Just down the hall from Regan's office were the people who not only knew about the project but had contributed much of their time to it. Regan, however, was adamant about the secrecy, and he directed Chrystie to inform the employees that they would be fired if they mentioned the project to anyone outside the company. This seemed a peculiar way to express appreciation for the time they had put in. Chrystie suggested that he thank the employees and appeal to their sense of pride in the effort to keep it secret. Regan bristled. "We'll do it your way, but it had better work," he said after a pause.

In the fall of 1977, Merrill began offering the Cash Management Account in Columbus, Atlanta, and Athens, Georgia, and in Denver and Boulder. The Colorado locations proved something of a Waterloo, because the bankers there were enraged by the Merrill Lynch invasion. The securities giant was seen as the big-city adventurer, arrogant and disrespectful of local custom. The Colorado State Banking Board sued the firm, charging that it was engaged in unlicensed banking, and the Colorado bankers threatened to stir up big trouble for Merrill Lynch across the country. Small bankers are active conventioneers. The outraged Coloradans used every opportunity to foment opposition to the CMA in other states. In Oregon, for example, where Merrill Lynch was planning to expand with the CMA, John Olin, the state's superintendent of banks, made the astute appraisal that the Cash Management Account "looked like a duck, walked like a duck, and quacked like a duck." That being the case, he reasoned, it should be regulated by whoever was charged with regulating ducks. Merrill Lynch, unamused, decided to steer clear of Oregon. However, Olin's homey analogy became the battle cry of hundreds of small banks all over the country. Not to be hoodwinked by fancy nomenclature, they decried the CMA as a thinly disguised, unregulated banking service.

In one respect, the bankers were right: customers would use the CMA as a surrogate bank account. It offered the convenience of instant liquidity and instant credit while providing a yield superior to that offered by traditional savings vehicles. It had the advantages of a savings account, a checking account, and a credit line. But the bankers were wrong on one point: though customers might use the CMA as they would a bank account, or even empty out a bank account to set up a CMA, Merrill Lynch could not treat the CMA monies as a bank could treat deposits. Funds placed in CMA accounts couldn't be lent or invested by Merrill Lynch. They remained the assets of the account-holder and had to be invested in shares of a money fund, which was itself invested in short-term debt securities, as set out in a prospectus.

Merrill Lynch was encountering problems not only with bankers but with the people it had counted among its most vital supporters — its own brokers. Most were brought up in an investment world that consisted of stocks and bonds. The new financial service required different procedures and explanations. In addition, the product didn't bring a sales commission for the broker, as did most other transactions.

In January 1978, the cynicism felt toward the embattled Cash Management Account was given voice at an annual luncheon where Merrill Lynch executives set aside their self-congratulations and engaged in an orgy of mutual derision. Behind the head table was a flag with the familiar Merrill

Lynch bull, but beneath the proud animal was a heap of excrement. After the usual toasting and banter, the time came to make the annual presentation of the Merrill Lynch Golden Turd Award to the executive believed to have created the greatest mess for the company during the year. The scato-logical ceremony even had a trophy of sorts — an amorphous heap sprayed gold and mounted on a wooden plaque. The award went to Tom Chrystie, father of the Cash Management Account, seemingly the biggest disaster the firm had dreamed up in some years.

During 1979, after a lackluster response in the test markets, Merrill Lynch began to offer brokers bonuses for CMA sales. Those who opened the most accounts got free trips to Hawaii or Puerto Rico. Around this time, things began to improve for the CMA. Merrill Lynch agreed, after Herculean nego-tiations, to several limitations on its account in Colorado that finally reconciled the bankers to a grudging coexistence with the new competitor. The entire fracas had succeeded in giving Merrill Lynch an edge over its Wall Street competitors, who understandably decided to wait on the sidelines and let Merrill Lynch fight the legal battle with the banks. As a result, Merrill Lynch enjoyed four years of monopoly in the service. Regan had figured the firm could count on no more than six months of exclusive franchise.

Another development that played right into Merrill Lynch's hands was the worsening economy. The rate of inflation surged upward in 1978 and again in 1979. With the Iranian revolu-tion, an already ragged economy was slugged with steep increases in oil prices. Corporate earnings slumped badly. Equity markets became demoralized, and the staid bond mar-kets were shoved onto a roller coaster by veering interest rates. People weren't sure where things were going. The confusing state of affairs produced a pervasive tentativeness. Investors wanted their money to be in the most liquid format possible without leaving themselves open to the ravages of the inflation. Short-term interest rates were soaring, and the money funds were bulging with new customers.

The billions started rolling in, and in volume that surprised Merrill Lynch's most bullish optimists. The strange hybrid of a financial service — called a bank, a duck, an investment account, a line of credit — proved more attractive than anyone had anticipated. As CMA money poured in, Merrill Lynch found itself packing more and more people into servicing the program. It was clear that consumers had changed. Before, personal financial management had concentrated on providing the consumer with income, as well as a degree of safety and the prospect of growth. Now, a new factor had begun to dominate the mind of the average investor — protection against inflation. It was as if a stranger had invaded the territory of financial services and begun to deride the plans of all the others as being inadequate for protecting assets against inflation. People moved toward term life policies in droves. Those with maturing whole life policies began borrowing against them at irrationally low rates in order to buy products before prices jumped higher or in order to realize a greater gain elsewhere. The old products were losing favor, and new ones, relying on the computer, were drawing attention and money. The Cash Management Account showed itself to be a product that fitted the needs of consumers. As others scrambled to compete, it became clear that the CMA had permanently changed the business of big financial companies. The traditional definitions and rules were blurring, and the game had become not banking or brokerage, but capturing assets.

8

At the end of 1977, Sandy Lewis left the crowded, drab quarters of the Securities and Exchange Commission, where he had been an adviser to Chairman Harold Williams, and became part of one of Wall Street's most powerful and mysterious subcultures, the specialty business of arbitrage. Lewis had already been involved in arbitrage at other points in his career, most recently at Merrill Lynch, where he had set up a small department dedicated to this specialized form of trading. The main basis for arbitrage in the late 1970s and early 1980s was corporate mergers, in which a company trading at $25 a share might be taken over for $40 a share a month later. The growth in corporate mergers created a boom in merger-related investments for Wall Street trading rooms. In 1975, corporate mergers carried an aggregate value of $11.8 billion. In 1978, the amount had ballooned to $34.2 millon. Arbitrageurs, who were understandably proliferating on Wall Street, tried to identify likely merger targets or guess the outcome of current takeover battles. When companies got scooped up for more than the market price, they raked in massive profits. When they guessed wrong, their losses could be equally stupendous.

Like Merrill Lynch, many of the big Wall Street firms — including Salomon Brothers, Smith Barney Harris Upham, Morgan Stanley, and Goldman Sachs — operated thickly capitalized arbitrage departments. There was also an increase in the number of small firms specializing in arbitrage. Most didn't take on outside customers; they put together several million dollars in partners' capital and sought to make the sum grow by betting on the takeovers. The dean of the arbitrageurs, and founder of the first major arbitrage partnership, was Ivan Boesky, and it was his firm, Boesky & Company, that Lewis decided to join in late 1977.

Boesky, the son of a Detroit milkman, was trained as a lawyer and accountant and had run the arbitrage department at Edwards & Hanly before establishing his own firm in 1975. This he did with $700,000 from his wife, Seema, whose father, Ben Silverstein, owned the Beverly Hills Hotel and other high-priced properties around the United States. Boesky also had a talent for attracting money from outside the family. He aggressively publicized his triumphs and was featured in *Fortune* magazine in 1977 for having made a killing in the stock of Babcock & Wilcox, which was acquired by United Technologies. Partners drawn to the firm over the years included such big-dollar investors as Eli Broad, chairman of Kaufman & Broad, Mortimer Zuckerman, real estate entrepreneur and owner of the *Atlantic* magazine, and Robin Farkas, chairman of Alexander's department store. Five years after it was launched, Boesky & Company had capital of about $90 million as a result of added investments and retained profits.

Boesky was also intent on attracting talent to his firm. He undertook a protracted courtship of Sandy Lewis in 1977, when the latter was working at the SEC. The two men had met each other several years earlier, when Boesky sought a job at Merrill Lynch. Because of Boesky's individualistic and entrepreneurial nature, Lewis thought it unlikely that he'd fit in with the corporate culture at Merrill Lynch and had said as much to Don Regan. Boesky went on to build his own arbitrage house.

There was much in Boesky that Lewis found compelling. He was smart and fiercely independent. Like Lewis, he refused to operate by the conventional rules of decorum in the financial business, sometimes antagonizing the powerful and respected investment bankers on Wall Street. Boesky, often called "the mad Russian," was an outsider, a black sheep, a loner. And this, too, appealed to Lewis.

In late 1977, Lewis borrowed some money from his father and set up a partnership account in Boesky & Company in Barbara's name. Soon afterward, he became a general partner in the firm.

For Lewis, who was nearly obsessed with understanding things, arbitrage was a satisfying discipline. Takeover deals were mysteries to be unraveled, one after another. For each deal, there were dozens of aspects to analyze: What was the value of assets owned by the target in relation to the proposed takeover price? What was its future earning power? What were the personalities of the people involved in the takeover battle? Which side was the more likely to cave in if things got nasty?

When takeover offers were mentioned, the arbitrageurs plied the telephone nonstop, seeking information. They dispatched lawyers to determine whether there might be antitrust violations; accountants to grind through the quarterly financial disclosures. If there were court proceedings in a contested takeover, the arbitrage houses would station people in the courtrooms, their pockets bulging with change so that they could rush to pay phones and relay news back to the trading desks. The arbitrageurs — known in the vernacular as "the arbs" — lived on the merger frenzy, following each merger drama hour by hour, gossiping over the telephone with one another, constantly assessing and reassessing their trading positions.

The investment patterns of the arbs varied from one take-over to the next. In a clear-cut case, where the takeover target was almost certain to be acquired at a price above its market value, the arbs would swoop in to buy up stock in the target company. This would, of course, be sold to the acquirer later at a profit. There were embellishments to each investment, such as the use of options to offset some of the risk. By contrast, if a stock had been run up on the generally held expectation of a takeover, and the arbs learned that it would not take place, they would unload shares they held in the takeover target or sell short. Overall, the business offered grist for Lewis' analytical talents and fed his zest for urgent and immediate action.

The business worried him, too. Among other things, there was a peculiar symbiosis between the arbitrageurs who bet on the deals and the investment bankers who engineered them. Corporate mergers had created more than trading opportunities for Wall Street; they had given rise to large advisory fees for the investment banks who marshaled the corporations through the takeover wars. Lazard Frères, under the stewardship of André Meyer, had been a leading strategist behind many of the big mergers of the sixties. Morgan Stanley had built up a fee-hungry merger department in the seventies. And Salomon Brothers, Goldman Sachs, and First Boston were quick to do the same. Whether the merger craze ben-efited the American economy one jot, it was a boon for Wall Street — both for its corporate advisers and its cadre of merger speculators, the arbitrageurs. These two groups were often in a position to help one another. The arbs were perpetually hungry for information on what was happening behind the scenes in a takeover. The investment bankers — with whom they were friendly — were an important source of this in-formation. When, say, Morgan Stanley was leading the charge as an adviser in a particular takeover battle, the arbs deluged Robert Greenhill, Morgan's top takeover strategist, with phone calls. Generally, the investment bankers enjoyed discussing with the arbitrageurs the war games they employed. (If a firm was acting as a paid adviser in a takeover situation, its own arbitrage department couldn't speculate lawfully as a trader in that takeover, because it had an assumed advantage.)

Likewise, the arbs were useful to the investment bankers; they could make deals happen. If, say, 30 percent or more of a company's shares fell into the hands of the arbs — and this wasn't uncommon — a would-be acquirer could feel as-sured that those shares would be for sale at the highest avail-able price, even if the management of the company was opposed to the acquisition. Individual shareholders often felt loyal to the management of a company. Thus, an investment banker serving a would-be acquirer could make the completion of a merger more likely by encouraging the arbs to stake out a substantial trading position in the takeover target.

Some officials were troubled that certain information that got passed on was classified as "inside information" under the securities laws. It was information that would affect the price of a stock, and it wasn't available to the public. Trading on the lucrative secrets was illegal and in 1981 became an enforcement priority for the SEC. Nonetheless, the use of inside information remained widespread and difficult to track down. Although the SEC never launched an action against a member of the arbitrage community, some Wall Street officials viewed the arbs as frequent perpetrators of insider-trading violations. Studies indicated, for example, that in a majority of the takeovers, the stocks of the target companies shot up in price just before the announcement of the planned merger, suggesting that some investors routinely knew about deals in advance.

In January 1981, a federal indictment detailed the orchestrations of a pair of former Morgan Stanley merger experts — Jacques Courtois and Adrian Antoniu — who had illegally peddled takeover secrets to outside traders, then pocketed a share of the resulting trading profits themselves. It was a gravely embarrassing episode for Morgan Stanley. Although Wall Street leaders roundly condemned the scheme, the machinations of Courtois and Antoniu were not inconsistent with a Wall Street culture that was increasingly attuned to "deal profits." "There but for the grace of God go I," said the top investment banker with another major firm, suggesting that the Morgan Stanley scandal could have occurred just as easily at his shop, given the profit-hungry business school graduates employed there.

Not wanting to give themselves away to rivals, or perhaps to regulators, many of the arbs disguised their buying through the use of filters. Boesky, the most closely watched, would usually route his orders through at least two brokers and a bank before they reached the floor. "Ivan likes a beard when he trades," one arb explained. Nonetheless, the grapevine on Wall Street operated with stunning efficiency, so when Boesky's orders arrived circuitously on the Exchange floor, arbs in different offices in New York would whisper, "Boesky's buying" or "Boesky's selling" some particular stock. When the filtering system became well known, Boesky would change the "beard."

Lewis' one-year stint at Ivan Boesky's arbitrage house wasn't a happy one. He had problems with Boesky's secrecy and his intensity. And though Lewis had thought he'd enjoy both independence and some managerial seniority at the firm, he believed that his actual treatment fell short of what had been promised. Significantly, Lewis wasn't given his own office, but was placed at a desk in a hallway beneath a huge swordfish Boesky had mounted on a wall.

Ivan Boesky was driven and egotistical. The turnover at his arbitrage house was nothing short of phenomenal. An article by Chris Welles in *Institutional Investor* gave this account of Boesky's management style:

> Given to ferocious outbursts of temper, he drove himself, his employees and his outside sources mercilessly to root out even the most minuscule facets of a deal. Monthly strategy meetings lasted from the early evening to 2 A.M. Once, when business was still pending, Boesky adjourned and ordered everyone to reconvene at 5 A.M.
>
> Some people couldn't stand his frantic pace and obsessive control. "He's a user of people," says one former partner. "He'd never admit anyone else contributed anything. His idea of a compliment was to say, 'You think just like I do.' "

There were other strains for Sandy at this time. Cy Lewis had severe health problems. Those close to Cy Lewis saw his final years as tragic. The old man remained physically imposing, although the once-handsome face was puffy and creased. He suffered from heart disease and disorders related to smoking. He was exhausted and played out, a tortured giant, bellicose but sad. At Bear Stearns, he would growl instructions to a subordinate, only to have Alan Greenberg, the top trader, come along and explain that the old man's directives should be ignored.

There was no question but that the firm would be left to

Greenberg's direction. He was already running it in many respects. Greenberg's mind was often compared to a computer. Where Lewis was moved by his own passions and appetites, Greenberg was poker-faced and apparently emotionless. He brought a sense of discipline to money-making. Cy Lewis, Greenberg once explained, had the problem of "falling in love with stocks," which meant that he was prey to the danger of hanging on to losing stocks. Cy Lewis found Greenberg cold. "He pees icewater," Lewis said of him. Nevertheless, Lewis decided to pass the mantle to Greenberg. By this time, the formal ritual of succession was simply a ratification of the modus operandi at Bear Stearns. No one was quite certain what Lewis would do afterward. Bear Stearns partners expected him to prowl about their offices, although his role would be negligible. He had spoken to Sandy about his dread of falling into his "dotage." Indeed, he had no interests or sources of enjoyment other than sports events and stock-trading.

The formal transfer of power came at the annual partners' dinner, held at the Harmonie Club on April 27, 1978. The club itself, where the Bear Stearns partners had taken to holding their annual dinners, was a place that must have carried some painful associations for Lewis. It had rejected Cy Lewis for membership in the 1960s, although it accepted him later, after Sandy intervened on his father's behalf.

Cy Lewis' retirement as a senior partner wasn't a particularly sentimental occasion. Bear Stearns was populated by tough money-makers not given to emotional outpourings; moreover, many of the Bear Stearns partners had been bullied by Lewis over the years and were just as glad to see him leave.

Still, it was the end of an era for the firm; Cy Lewis was the man who had turned the place into a financial powerhouse. A colleague, John Slade, presented Lewis with a watch that Lewis had seen and admired while in Switzerland on a business trip. If a watch seemed an oddly pedestrian gift for so unusual an entrepreneur, it may have been because Lewis' partners didn't know what else to give him. Lewis had no affection for possessions: there was nothing he collected or cherished.

After accepting the gift, Lewis returned to his seat, took the knife at his place setting, and began cutting the ribbon around the package. Moments later, his arms began moving back and forth over the table. One Bear Stearns partner remembered that Lewis looked as though he were a drowning man trying to swim. He never got to the watch inside the package. Two days later, Cy Lewis died at Mount Sinai Hospital. He had suffered a massive stroke at the Harmonie Club, followed by a series of strokes in the hospital.

The *New York Times* led its obituary page with news of the death, aptly recalling the awesome physical impact of Cy Lewis, "a huge man with a powerful voice." The *Times* story noted that Lewis had transformed Bear Stearns from a minor securities firm with less than $1 million in capital to a major Wall Street power with more than $50 million. Recalling Lewis' pioneering efforts in block-trading and his tough style, the obituary quoted a press interview in which Lewis said he had no interest in trying to relax at the close of the trading day. "I like tension," he had said.

Sandy arranged for a memorial service at Temple Emanu-El, on East Sixty-fifth Street, the one religious institution with which Cy Lewis had had an affiliation. (He had joined it only because the presidency of the Federation of Jewish Philanthropies had virtually required a temple membership. Once he relinquished that post, Lewis had allowed the membership to lapse.) On May 5, the central hall of the temple was brimming. Bear Stearns emptied out for the occasion. Sandy remembered a group of telephone operators from the firm clustered together close to the aisle, sobbing throughout the service. Rod Hills, the former Securities and Exchange Commission chairman, delivered a short eulogy. Financing clients and trading cronies were there by the hundreds. Some talked together about Cy, his impact on the business, the tortured quality of his last years. But before long, the conversations turned to the business Cy Lewis had left, to the stock market or the latest trend in the commission discounts the banks and pension funds were exacting from Wall Street.

As Sandy Lewis reflected on the day, an odd point of trivia came to him: there had been more people at Cy Lewis' memorial service than at the one held in 1977 for his rival, Gustave Levy of Goldman Sachs. It was an observation that his father, ever competitive, wouldn't have wanted overlooked.

A generation of financiers was disappearing. The same year as Cy Lewis' death, Billy Salomon stepped down as managing partner of Salomon Brothers. John Gutfreund, a syndicate expert (he had interviewed Sandy for his first job), assumed the position. Throughout the securities business, a new elite was gaining power, made up of people who had had their first taste of success during the freewheeling 1960s. Good times awaited them. There would be unprecedented trading volume, frenetic merger activity, and record levels of underwritings.

For Sandy Lewis, the immediate task was to extricate himself from Boesky & Company, the sixth firm he had worked for on Wall Street and the sixth where his expectations had been disappointed.

In December 1978, Sandy left the company and began exploring the prospect of teaching a course in mergers and arbitrage at Columbia Business School. It would be the chance to be around a university, which he thought he would enjoy, and to focus on the theoretical aspects of the securities business. His attempt to find some personal equilibrium on Wall Street, let alone establish a successful career there, had failed six times. He was still known chiefly as Cy Lewis' brash, mercurial son. Although teaching had some appeal to Lewis, he feared that a university might seem soporific after a while.

He had considerable responsibilities as the executor of his father's estate, which was valued at about $11 million, and was also in charge of managing the financial affairs of the family, including his siblings'.

In January of 1979, Sandy left on a trip to Israel that had been organized by a group of Jewish business people and professional men. Himself the son of a Jewish father and a Gentile mother, Sandy was again the outsider, the one who didn't entirely fit in.

The trip had its physical difficulties, too. Shortly after arriving in Tel Aviv, Lewis fell while trying to take a photograph from a mountaintop. He cracked bones in his elbow, briefly passed out, cut open his chin, and smashed his camera. As he lay recovering in a hospital in Tel Aviv, he began thinking more seriously than ever before about setting up a small company of his own.

Before leaving Israel, Sandy telephoned André Meyer, now retired from Lazard Frères. Meyer was himself a sort of mythical Wall Street figure, once described by Felix Rohatyn as "an Olympian figure, Zeus hurling thunderbolts." Meyer was representative of the disappearing generation of forceful and highly individualistic financiers who had dominated life on Wall Street in the postwar years; others in it were Robert Lehman, Billy Salomon, Gustave Levy, and of course Cy Lewis.

Meyer was also one of the early impresarios of the merger game. During the sixties, long before the big Wall Street merger factories had taken shape at First Boston and Morgan Stanley, Lazard was engineering the biggest mergers and acquisitions in the corporate arena. With Meyer operating as the chief architect, Lazard had played a central role in the conglomerating of American corporations. The firm had engineered McDonnell Company's acquisition of Douglas Aircraft, Atlantic Richfield's purchase of Sinclair Oil, and RCA's purchase of Hertz and, later, Random House.

Meyer, who was living in Crans, just outside Geneva, said that he would be happy to have Sandy visit. He had been a respected colleague of Cy Lewis and had long had a particular affection for Sandy. In Switzerland, Sandy explained to Meyer that he had a dream of setting up his own company. The firm would begin as an arbitrage house, speculating on takeovers. It would then move into merger-making itself so that it didn't have to bet only on deals that others engineered. And Lewis told Meyer that the first deal he had in mind was the marriage of American Express and Shearson Loeb Rhoades.

Meyer listened carefully. He then told Sandy that he felt he should never work for another firm and should certainly use his energy and intelligence to set up his own. Meyer believed Lewis could make a success of it. He also said he would be willing to put up $500,000 to become a limited partner in the firm.

The two men took a walk on a mountain ridge not far from Meyer's home. Meyer was dying of cancer of the prostate, and in the sharp winter light his face had a sickly, ashen cast. Sandy took two photographs of Meyer near his home and said he would be in touch with him about his role in the partnership. Meyer never became a partner. He died on September 9, 1979.

But there would be others willing to put up money. Meyer had given Lewis something more important: a sort of paternal blessing, coming, if not from his actual father, then from his father's generation. By the time of Meyer's death, S. B. Lewis & Company was well on its way to being set up.

*　*　*

When Lewis returned from his trip to Israel and his visit with André Meyer, he was brimming with enthusiasm about creating his own securities firm. Almost immediately after getting home, he met Jim Robinson of American Express for breakfast at the River Club. Driving in to New York from Short Hills that morning, with an almost blinding sun pouring in from the East, Lewis had a stark realization. "I want Jim Robinson to give me a new life," he told himself. Specifically, he wanted Robinson to invest money in the firm that he, Lewis, would set up, and to give that firm the go-ahead to act as marriage broker in the merger of American Express and Shearson Loeb Rhoades.

If Robinson said yes to both suggestions, there would indeed be a new life for Lewis, at least a new life on Wall Street. There would be a chance to obliterate a reputation for being just the brash, volatile son of a successful tycoon. To bring American Express into the securities business would change things for Wall Street irrevocably.

Although American Express had its headquarters near Wall Street, it remained outside the clubby enclave. It was less colorful, less feverish, and much, much bigger than any securities firm in the United States, including Merrill Lynch. The world of American Express was symbolized by a six-story glass and concrete structure in Plantation, Florida. This was one of three huge data-processing plants that stood behind the vast empire of American Express. Rising above a scrubby, semitropical landscape in southern Florida, the place had the appropriately futuristic acronym of SROC, for Southern Regional Operating Center. Inside were cool, well-lit rooms and a battery of modern data-processing equipment: 33,000 reels of magnetic tapes, acres of computers, optical readers for the credit card transactions, laser printers capable of whipping out 20,000 lines a minute.

The twenty-eight hundred employees at the Florida data-processing center worked with robotlike efficiency. One room of workers, mostly women, spent the days and nights answering telephone calls from merchants around the world asking about particular credit card customers. Computers monitored the length of time it took operators to answer each call — 2.6 seconds was an average that pleased one foreman. Other computers were used to hunt out the workers who were slowing down the average if it inched up to an unacceptable level of, say, 3.5 seconds. Once the slowpokes were located, they'd be temporarily removed to a "training corner," where their timing would be monitored closely. When they began answering within an acceptable period, they would be allowed to return to the larger room.

In another room was a phalanx of computers logging information on people who steal American Express cards, ignore their bills, or cheat the system in other ways.

American Express, begun in 1850 as a carrier company, had assets of more than $20 billion and was, in some ways, a vast data-processing company. With its twelve million cardholders and its millions of traveler's check customers, it played a middleman role in the payment for goods and services. Lewis believed that American Express should also start playing a role in the investment of money and that it should accomplish this by buying a piece of Wall Street. The American Express card could be the principal means of giving people quick access to funds in their investment accounts.

Lewis also thought that the acquisition of a Wall Street firm would be a good thing for his old friend Robinson, who, in three years as chairman of American Express, had stubbed his toes on a string of unsuccessful merger attempts with Disney World, the Book-of-the-Month Club, and Philadelphia Life Insurance. Lewis recognized that Sandy Weill, by contrast, had a proven track record of making mergers happen, so if he was brought into the executive suite at American Express, he might be able to change things there.

Lewis' breakfast with Robinson at the River Club was a disappointment. Robinson was preoccupied with another takeover attempt — his firm's unwelcome bid for McGraw-Hill. Harold McGraw's tenacious efforts to thwart the acquisition were beginning to make American Express look like a clumsy, arrogant predator. Robinson seemed powerless to reverse the impression.

Lewis talked during the breakfast about why American Express should avoid a nasty takeover battle with McGraw-Hill and focus its energies on a friendly merger with a Wall Street firm, namely, Shearson Loeb Rhoades. Robinson idly mentioned the prospect of buying Merrill Lynch. (Don Regan, it turned out, had suggested the possibility of combining Merrill Lynch and American Express to Robinson a couple of years earlier, but the talks hadn't progressed much past the hypothetical. Among other things, the tight antitrust policies of the mid-1970s could well have precluded such a combination.) With respect to the idea of sinking money into a new investment firm organized and managed by Lewis, Robinson was interested but noncommittal.

Lewis rented an office at Bear Stearns, his father's old firm, and began working to create his own company. He spoke with lawyers, researched the type of structure needed for a partnership, and talked to wealthy acquaintances who might be interested in putting up money and becoming limited partners in the company. He contacted many of his father's old business cronies, but most found reasons for steering clear of the partnership. Few doubted Lewis' intelligence and ability, but his bumpy Wall Street career was reason for concern. Negotiations proceeded slowly. In January 1980, American Express agreed to put in $4 million from a special investment portfolio within the company. The amount was a crucial sum to Lewis, but it represented only a pittance to the gigantic

American Express. Another $2 million came from Diana Lewis and from some smaller pockets in the Lewis family. A few other big names decided to join in. Roderick Hills, the one-time Securities and Exchange Commission chairman who had spoken at Cy Lewis' funeral, and his wife, Carla, the former Housing and Urban Development Secretary, each put in funds. Harold Williams, the SEC chief for whom Lewis had worked, also became a limited partner.

Cy Lewis' legacy helped the new firm in several respects. A portion of his fortune had gone into seeding the younger Lewis' nascent firm. In addition, Sandy Lewis persuaded the telephone operators at Bear Stearns to pass on to him his father's source lists, which comprised names and numbers of financiers and business people all over the world. Since Sandy planned to enter the arbitrage business, well-placed people on these lists could provide vital information on what was happening in the merger battles Lewis would bet on. "This telephone list alone was worth millions," Lewis once said.

Lewis also began talking selectively with a handful of people he wanted to work with him. Neil Goldstein, a soft-spoken, witty analyst from Lehman Brothers Kuhn Loeb, began riding into Wall Street with Lewis from New Jersey and talking about a job at the new firm. On these commutes, Lewis would speak about the arbitrage business and about his ultimate desire to be a matchmaker for Shearson and American Express. Goldstein, like others Lewis sought out, visited Lewis at home to meet his family. What he saw made him realize that the values of Lewis' embryonic firm, S. B. Lewis & Company, would be different from those which prevailed at many Wall Street houses. "Our work isn't our life," Goldstein said. "That was what really impressed me about Sandy. He really cared about his wife and kids. I've been married thirteen years, first wife and all that. I get a lot of excitement out of making money on these deals, but I also get a lot of excitement at seeing a child crawl across a rug."

Lewis found office space for his new firm at 76 Beaver Street, a narrow side street in the Wall Street area. He set up the offices for the eight-person firm with careful attention to décor and to ambience. Fresh flowers were brought in every other day; pictures were selected by Lewis. His own office was dominated by a brooding self-portrait of Eastman Johnson. The painting, completed in the artist's last years, suggests the pathos of old age, with the figure half sunk in black shadows. The eyes, almost totally obscured, have a charred, ghostly appearance. The painting is a reminder of the painful regrets of old age — regrets that Cy Lewis felt acutely in his last years.

S. B. Lewis & Company bet money on takeovers and traded stocks on a modest scale throughout the summer of 1980. Then Sandy set up the breakfast meeting with Sandy Weill and Jim Robinson and went to work mating Shearson Loeb Rhoades and American Express, the deal he believed would redeem his Wall Street career.

Following the meeting at American Express Tower, where Weill met Robinson for the first time, Lewis realized he would have to provide the momentum, or the talks would fizzle. Although neither Robinson nor Weill was willing to dismiss the idea of a merger, neither was committed to it. Lewis had to rely on his own enormous drive — and on the telephone. For Sandy Lewis the telephone was an extension of his personality. It was an instrument of intervention: he could catch people just after they got out of bed, arrived at their offices, or reached home in the evening, and for at least a short period of time he could press his views on them. And he could control the timing and frequency of the telephone conversations. Lewis became a constant caller to Weill and Robinson. He learned their schedules — what time each got to work and left, what time each tended to get going in the morning. He decided that he would simply proceed as though the two corporate chairmen had instructed him to put together the merger. They hadn't, of course, but they hadn't pushed him away, either.

The drawbacks of a merger were obvious. Weill and others at Shearson found American Express to be a bureaucratic place, where executives seemed to spend hours writing dull memos defending their own jobs. Robinson had his own worries. After Merrill Lynch had created its Cash Management Account — a move Shearson and others planned to imitate — Wall Street had moved into banklike services. Billions were pouring out of bank accounts into high-yielding instruments set up by the securities firms. For the securities houses, the friction with the banks was part of the normal competition for individuals' funds. But Robinson had to view the situation a little differently. He depended on thousands of banks around the country to distribute American Express traveler's checks. If those banks began to view American Express as a competitor because it owned a securities firm, they might decide to curtail this distribution, to the detriment of the American Express check business.

There was also much volatility in the securities business. Despite the diversifications firms had embarked on, the profits of the brokerage businesses shriveled as the stock market slumped. During the fall of 1980, Lewis' persistence notwithstanding, Robinson told Sandy that American Express just wasn't interested in the deal. He explained that the banks might become angry and that this could impair the traveler's check business. Lewis replied defiantly, "I've heard your reasons. They don't stand up, and you are going to do it."

But Lewis needed help in moving Robinson toward the merger table. As it happened, a conflict brewing a few blocks away from American Express headquarters was to have a profound effect on Robinson's ultimate decision. It was taking place at Bache Group, Inc.

9

The effect of the 1970s on Bache was the opposite of what it was on Shearson. During this turbulent period, Shearson achieved the much-contested status of second largest securities house in the country. (It was tacitly assumed on Wall Street that Merrill Lynch, Pierce, Fenner & Smith, Inc., was and always would be the largest.) Bache, for its part, began the decade as number two but slid to seventh place by the time the seventies were ended. As Shearson saw its prowess grow, Bache saw its reputation fade and its name on Wall Street stand for bungling mediocrity. Profit margins at Bache lagged behind not only those at Shearson but those at nearly every other large national securities firm that survived the 1970s' shakeout. Many Bache stockbrokers left to take jobs at other firms. Those who stayed produced measurably less in commissions than brokers at Shearson, Merrill Lynch, E. F. Hutton, and Paine Webber, to name a few large rivals.

And yet Bache endured. Though it came close to insolvency in 1970 in the wake of the paperwork crisis — which hit Bache hard — and long afterward was rumored to be a takeover candidate, Bache managed both to keep its independence and to recover its profitability, though at modest levels. The firm exhibited a sort of animal stamina that enabled it to cling to its shrunken turf on the Street, despite all expectations to the contrary.

At the center of the firm was the tenacious Harry A. Jacobs, who had spent a career at Bache and risen to the chairmanship amid the countless political struggles the firm was known for. Jacobs fitted instinctively into the role of the defender, which was a good thing, for it seemed to be Bache's fate to be pushed to the wall repeatedly. Jacobs was neither an expansive nor an inventive financier, but he could fight prodigiously for his and Bache's survival. Harry Jacobs avoided both manner and actions that were daring or boldly entrepreneurial. He sought instead an identity for himself and his firm that was dependable and steady.

A Dartmouth graduate and former World War II Army Air Corps pilot, Jacobs arrived at Bache in 1946, two years after the company had lost its patriarch with the death of eighty-three-year-old Jules S. Bache. Jules Bache had been a man of considerable intelligence and flair in the world of investment banking and securities brokerage.

The heir apparent, by virtue of being the closest relative in the firm, was the financier's nephew, Harold Bache. Harold, who had joined the firm in 1914, had garnered little of his uncle's esteem during his years at Bache, and was remembered as being a dull man. When Jules Bache died, his will revealed some surprises. He bestowed his considerable assets on many — he made a gift of a $12.5 million trove of European art treasures to the Metropolitan Museum — but left only meager remembrances to Harold Bache and to the securities firm. In fact, Jules Bache's instructions were that his money be yanked out of the company soon after his death.

Harold Bache was determined to build back the firm. Lacking access to family wealth, he began to scrape for capital among prospective partners and succeeded in coming up with $4 million by June 1945. This was sufficient for him to begin setting up new branch offices around the country. He later reopened the overseas offices that had been boarded up during the war. The company started to grow. It was a good time to be in the securities business; firms were beginning to participate in the postwar expansion and in the accumulation of wealth by America's vast middle class.

The young Harry Jacobs became "Harold Bache's little boy," according to a close associate. He worked in sales, investment research, and syndicates before moving into the general management of the firm in the 1950s. Jacobs grew fiercely proud of the legacy Harold Bache had managed not only to preserve but to build on, and he was deeply loyal to the man who acted as his mentor and advocate at the firm.

Another play for power came in April 1972, four years after Harold Bache's death, and was known within the firm as "the night of the long knives." In a decisive move, Jacobs managed to wrest from Edward O'Brien, chairman of Bache's executive committee, the management responsibility for retail and institutional brokerage. These were the bread-and-butter operations of the firm. With them neatly tucked under his control, Jacobs enjoyed a clear passage to the chairmanship. O'Brien remained at Bache a while longer; he left in April 1974 to become the president of the Securities Industry Association, Wall Street's major trade group.

Harry Jacobs — a man of average height, balding, with large blue eyes and a toothy grin — became Bache's chief executive officer and, later, chairman of the board, as well. His demeanor was genial and pleasant, but he was fiercely protective of his company. Once, when Morgan Stanley's president, Robert H. B. Baldwin, telephoned Jacobs to tell him, out of politeness, that he had hired one of the Bache vice presidents, Jacobs blurted, "You can't do that!" and hung up on the revered Morgan chief. He then bested Morgan's offer, and the vice president stayed.

Jacobs viewed himself as the steward of a valuable inheritance at Bache. Although the new breed that came to Wall Street in the sixties showed little reverence for historical rankings, Jacobs attached significance to the sheer stretch of history behind him. It was of surpassing importance to him that the firm was a hundred years old. In October 1979, Bache celebrated its centennial with a sumptuous luncheon at the Hotel Pierre. Top executives from leading brokerage houses, banks, and money management firms were invited. A silver coin with Bache's name and its dates, 1879–1979, was given to each guest. Smiling out at the filled ballroom, Harry Jacobs stated proudly from the dais that "of the tens of thousands of American corporations now operating, there are relatively few that can trace their origins back to the year 1879. Among those whose history began the same year as ours are the Scott Paper Company, the Mennen Company, the F. W. Woolworth Company, and our Wall Street friends Paine Webber." Jacobs went on to assure the community that Bache would be one of the survivors by the year 2000. "We will continue to be a major factor, whatever changes occur or whatever new directions are taken. We are absolutely determined to commit our resources, our manpower, and our skills to this end." When Jacobs spoke of Bache's position in the business, past or future, his voice took on a slightly brittle, defensive edge, as though these expressions of confidence were at least partly intended to negate the poor-relation treatment Bache was subjected to on Wall Street.

"You know," Jacobs said toward the end of his talk, "some years ago we commissioned an independent survey among investors to determine how they positioned Bache among other Wall Street firms. This survey showed that we were 'solid and dependable, like a bank.' I'm proud of this image, and I'm going to do my best to ensure that we retain it." This was a curious declaration for a Wall Street executive, because executives in the brokerage business felt their firms to be vastly different from — and often superior to — the banks. Wall Street was run by entrepreneurial energy, and even the more settled Wall Street types paid at least lip service to this practice. Banks were, in the eyes of most Wall Street executives, run by plodding bureaucrats who had no imaginative investment ideas.

Jacobs' aversion to an overtly aggressive approach kept his firm on the sidelines during most of the merger activity of the 1970s, when Sandy Weill was building a new empire on the wreckage of old Wall Street names. Bache had had discussions with the failing I. E. Du Pont Walston about acquiring some of its offices and with H. Hentz about a merger, but both projects fell through. Bache did buy Halsey Stuart, a solid underwriting house, in 1973, and Shields Model Roland, a major factor in the institutional brokerage trade, in 1977. Shields came to Bache after takeover talks with Shearson broke down. According to Weill, the sticking point was the exact role that would be filled by Virgil Sherrill, Shields's chief executive. Sherrill was a socially prominent investment man, with a smooth manner, sharp blue eyes, and silver hair. In the words of one colleague, "If M-G-M came to Wall Street looking for an investment banker type, they couldn't do much better than Virg." Weill found Sherrill to be "a nice

guy but not the hands-on type that would work out here."
Bache, on the contrary, promised Sherrill the presidency of
its flagship brokerage unit, Bache Halsey Stuart, so a merger
agreement was sealed there.

Neither the Halsey Stuart merger nor the Shields combination produced the desired results. Bache failed to communicate to the new people that the firm would reward their
particular skills. Many of them left. In the end, the Halsey
Stuart deal failed to establish Bache as a major underwriter.
Nor did the Shields merger make Bache a significant player
in the institutional brokerage game. Bache remained a big,
sprawling retail broker, and one of the least profitable, at
that.

By the late seventies, when corporate mergers were becoming a national pastime, Bache came to be identified as a
primary takeover candidate. Its stock was selling cheap — at
$7 or $8 a share — and despite its various problems, Bache
had the attraction of a national franchise of brokerage outlets.
Would-be acquirers figured that this network could someday
produce healthy profits.

The first serious assault occurred on May 17, 1978, when
Jerry Tsai, a Shanghai-born investment specialist, lowered a
helicopter onto a field adjacent to Jacobs' home in Westchester
County. It was a sporadically observed tradition that Tsai
and Jacobs would go on an outing in the helicopter, during
which Tsai would give the former Army Air Corps pilot a
lesson in hovering. The association between the two went
back to the 1950s, when Tsai had gotten his start on Wall
Street as an analyst at Bache, before emerging as one of the
virtuoso mutual fund managers during the 1960s.

But this time, instead of taking the helicopter to West
Point, as in the past, Tsai guided the craft to a small airfield
in New Jersey. Jacobs remembered the place as being "god-

forsaken." Tsai started the conversation by talking about some shareholders of Bache known as "the Brady-Schwartz group." Two of the men were metals dealers known in commodities circles: Ben Schwartz of Marshalltown, Iowa, and Eli Rosenman of Ottumwa, Iowa. The third, Harold S. Brady, a wealthy investor from Chicago, had recently died. But the three had accumulated 489,300 shares in Bache in 1974 and 1975 and had, on occasion, criticized the firm's management for the sluggish profitability. Otherwise, the group had been little more than interested investors. Now Brady's death had disturbed the status quo; there was speculation about where the shares might go. Before anything was resolved, Tsai had snapped up 70,700 shares. Then he began discussions with the remaining two principals. Altogether, Tsai and these outside investors controlled about 8 percent of the outstanding Bache shares.

Tsai explained all this to the stunned Bache chief executive and concluded by saying that he'd like to acquire a majority of the Bache shares and eventually become co-chairman of the company, alongside Jacobs. Tsai had long had ambitions of running a national financial empire, and Bache seemed the perfect opportunity for him. Jacobs listened, aghast, as the former analyst unveiled both his past actions and his intentions.

Then he gave his response: "I'm going to fight you to the death."

The trip back to Westchester through the thick drizzle was predictably tense. The helicopter descended to the wet grass in the field beside Jacobs' house. The Bache chief unloaded himself and began running. He crossed the field quickly, jumped over the fence at the edge of his yard, and continued running till he reached the house. He dashed for a telephone in the kitchen and rang up John Leslie, the current Bache chairman.

It took the two men only a few minutes to decide to seek the aid of Martin Lipton, senior partner of the law firm Wachtell, Lipton, Rosen & Katz and one of two recognized legal deans in the takeover game. (The other was Joseph Flom, of Skadden, Arps, Slate, Meagher & Flom.) Lipton was pre-eminent in defending corporations against acquisition-minded marauders. When Harold McGraw, the McGraw-Hill chairman, was fending off the unwanted takeover overtures from Jim Robinson at American Express, he sat, unannounced, in the reception area of Lipton's Park Avenue offices for an hour. Lipton had indicated that because of a pressing workload he couldn't handle the defense. McGraw was determined to convince him otherwise. He did, and Lipton engineered the successful defense that kept McGraw-Hill independent.

Lipton, a genial, bespectacled attorney with a calm, professorial manner, took on Bache in 1978 and began mapping a strategy to avert the outcome Tsai had forecast on the helicopter trip. Bache would buy back the shares accumulated by Tsai and the Brady-Schwartz group for $10.25 a share. That was about 20 percent higher than the market price. Lipton's plan was put into effect and was successful. Later, critics charged that Bache had put its other shareholders at a disadvantage, and the New York Stock Exchange and the Securities and Exchange Commission both launched investigations of the Brady-Schwartz buy-back. In the end, neither brought any action against Bache. For its part, the firm offered a rather confused justification for the stock purchase:

> The board voted to approve the purchase of these shares because it was in the best interest of the company. The belief of the board was that the holders of that stock had substantial policy interests with the Bache management. Mr. Tsai in early June had inferred [sic] that he had support of the Brady-Schwartz

block and talked about the possibility of a takeover. We felt that such an association wasn't in the best interests of Bache. Rumors of a takeover weren't doing us any good, and we were worried that the rumors could cost us a number of registered reps.

The buy-back succeeded in quelling the threat from Jerry Tsai, but it didn't end the rumors that Bache was going to be taken over. Moreover, the Tsai threat left Jacobs and others in Bache's management more preoccupied than ever with the prospect of being snatched up by a predator. As Wall Street moved into the relative bounty of 1979 — trading volume was rising and commissions were flowing in — Bache became an even more tempting catch. For the first time in more than a decade, it looked as though the major Wall Street firms were poised to make big money.

Harry Jacobs watched the action in Bache's shares closely after the Tsai affair. Whenever he sensed from the flickerings on his desktop computer that there was an active buyer in the market, he made a few calls to find out who the buyer was. Wall Street's redoubtable grapevine generally provided clues.

Not long after the Tsai threat, another takeover plan appeared. Jack Nash, the hard-driving chief of Oppenheimer & Company, approached Jim Robinson and several other top executives at American Express to suggest that the two join forces and make a tender offer for Bache shares. Given the low price of Bache's stock, the would-be acquirers could probably snap up the entire firm for less than $200 million, a bargain price. But the American Express people were cool to the idea. A modicum of research indicated that Bache would require a massive overhaul before it could function at a highly profitable level. Since American Express wasn't in the securities business, Robinson made it clear to Nash that it was the Oppenheimer people who would have to tend to the revamping job. This wasn't a task Nash wanted either, and the idea died quickly.

Then a spark of investor interest in Bache came from outside the United States. In late 1978, Virgil Sherrill learned from Peter Cundill, a Canadian investment adviser, that the Belzberg family of Western Canada, about whom Sherrill and Jacobs knew virtually nothing, were buying Bache shares. A few more telephone calls revealed that the family had built up a financial services' empire in Vancouver, after some successful ventures in real estate and energy. This intelligence seemed to be sufficient for the time being.

In March 1979, while Harry Jacobs was in Munich attending a meeting of business managers from around the world, he learned that a block of sixty thousand Bache shares had been sold. The Belzbergs were the buyers. Jacobs wanted to find out more about them and their objectives. Privately, he believed that the Canadian family intended to acquire control of Bache.

The impression was confirmed on March 21, when the Belzbergs filed with the Securities and Exchange Commission a Schedule 13-D disclosure statement, as required by the federal securities laws. The filing revealed that the Belzbergs' purchases far exceeded what the Wall Street grapevine had indicated. The family had acquired some 363,100 shares, or 5.1 percent of the outstanding common stock in Bache. The shares had been placed in a trio of Belzberg investment concerns, known as Bel-Fran Investments Ltd., Bel-Cal Holdings Ltd., and Bel-Alta Holdings Ltd. The stock purchases — which carried a total price of $3,002,687.55 — were largely financed by the Toronto Dominion Bank, which had extended a liberal line of credit to the Belzbergs. The Canadians were enigmatic, in their SEC filing, about how far they intended to go with their Bache purchases. For Harry Jacobs, however, there was no doubt now that the Canadians intended to seize control of the century-old securities house. At this point, Jacobs wrote the following into a small, black spiral notebook he always carried with him: "Buy up 15%. Tender for 51%. Put in new management, cut dividends, build up equity."

Jacobs had a yen for making predictions, remembering them, and alluding to them later. For example, he predicted in the late 1970s that there would soon be trading days of a hundred million shares on the New York Stock Exchange. When the magic day arrived, in August 1982, Jacobs issued a statement on the public relations news wire, reminding market observers that he had forecast the heavy trading several years earlier. The predictions regarding the Belzbergs' actions were, for Harry Jacobs, filled with dread. There was a legacy of steadfast independence at Bache. The firm had preserved its independence despite debilitating financial problems in the early 1970s. Jacobs had succeeded in staving off intrusion from Jerry Tsai and was determined to do the same with the Canadians. At the time Jacobs wrote the predictions in his black spiral notebook, he had no idea how many times he would refer to them over the next two years.

Four days after the SEC received the Belzbergs' first 13-D statement, the family sent off another. This one disclosed that the three Bel companies had acquired an additional forty-three thousand Bache shares, bringing the total stake to 406,100, or 5.7 percent of the company's outstanding stock. Four weeks later, another filing arrived at the commission, stating that the Bel companies had bought an additional 13,100 shares, for a total price of $112,158. Financing for the transaction had come through the line of credit extended by the Toronto Dominion Bank, as it had on the earlier purchases. In addition, the filing disclosed that John McAlduff, a top executive with Bel-Fran, had bought $20,000 worth of Bache stock for his personal account.

Around this time, Virgil Sherrill met with Samuel Belzberg, the leader of the clan and the chief executive of First City Financial, the Belzberg-controlled financial concern in Vancouver, at the New York Racquet Club. It was the first chance for the man controlling Bache's largest single block of stock to meet with the firm's management. It was also Bache's chance to communicate, through the polished and assured Sherrill, the management views on the stock purchases — namely, that for the general stability of the firm, its shareholders, and its customers, it would be best if the Belzbergs slowed down a bit in their purchases. On May 15, after about two weeks of quiet on the stock, Sherrill told Sam Belzberg over the telephone that he was pleased to see that the family hadn't upped its stake. According to a memo written later, "Mr. Belzberg made no response." Late the next month, there was another buying blitz, described in a 13-D filing sent to the SEC on July 3. This time, the Bel companies bought another 137,000 shares, for a total price of $1,392,970. This brought the Belzberg stake to 556,200 shares, or 7.8 percent of the company. The executive suite at Bache felt under siege. The Belzbergs seemed to have unlimited funds to deploy in the acquisition of Bache shares, and the steady accumulation was fast and strong. On September 13, Jacobs and Sherrill met Sam Belzberg in his suite at the Regency Hotel. This was Jacobs' first encounter with the Canadian; it was a tense session. Sam Belzberg was apparently eager to get involved in the United States financial services' business and was convinced that Bache represented the surest means of accomplishing this. As Jacobs sat in clenched silence, Belzberg explained that he foresaw the Bel companies expanding their stake to as much as 25 percent of Bache, either through purchases in the market or a partial tender offer for Bache shares. Furthermore, he left Sherrill and Jacobs with the correct impression that he would proceed regardless of their preferences. He did, however, express the hope that the Bache management would condone the purchases.

On September 24, 1979, Jacobs wrote to Belzberg that Bache viewed any increase in the Belzbergs' ownership as "contrary to the interests of Bache and its shareholders." Belzberg replied that "your letter misstates the essence of the discussions in my hotel suite." Again, he emphasized his hope that there could be "a spirit of cooperation."

The first major flurry of Belzberg purchases raised inside the old-line firm's ruling suite a major question: Just who were the Belzbergs? Harry Jacobs was a meticulously thorough executive, one given to copious preparations for every business encounter so that little could be left to chance. Convinced as he was that the Belzbergs intended not only to seize control of Bache but also to end his own position there, Jacobs spared no effort in researching the Canadian entrepreneurs and their past.

At first, Bache officials referred to this fact-gathering effort as "due diligence," employing the Wall Street vernacular for the routine economic investigation that any underwriter is obliged to undertake of a company whose shares it is selling to the public. But as the challenge from the Belzbergs grew more threatening, Bache's investigatory efforts turned into global espionage.

Bache pored initially over facts about the Belzbergs contained in the public record and called friends of Bache within the Canadian financial community. The family, it was learned, was hard-driving and immensely successful. Its net worth was estimated to be more than $500 million. By 1979, the Belzbergs appeared bent on emulating the leading financial dynasties of the United States by building wealth in energy, land, and industry, then converting it into a permanent position by creating a financial empire. Of greater concern to the Bache executives was the fact that the Belzbergs seemed to have outgrown Canada; more and more of their ventures were in the United States.

The brothers — Hyman, Samuel, and William — each managed a separate section of the family network of businesses but retained a share of ownership in all the ventures. Sam Belzberg was unquestionably the driving force behind the family's rapid accumulation of wealth and was the strategist of the move into the financial business. Hyman, the eldest, managed the family furniture company, Christy's Arcade Furniture Stores in Calgary, Alberta, and had little direct influence on the financial companies controlled by the family. The youngest brother, William, had been delegated by Sam to run Far West Financial, a Los Angeles–based savings and loan association the Belzbergs had gained control of in their expansion southward. The three brothers operated as equal partners, with each brother's interests placed in a separate Bel company. Bel-Alta represented Hyman's stake, Bel-Cal, Bill's, and Bel-Fran, Sam's. Alta was the abbreviation for Alberta, the province where Hyman lived and worked; Cal, of course, was the abbreviation for Bill's California base; and Fran was the name of Sam's wife, herself a Californian.

Orthodox Jews, the Belzberg brothers were the sons of Abraham Belzberg, who emigrated from Poland in 1919. He began peddling used furniture in western Canada. As the family grew, there came land dealings and, eventually, energy production. One of the biggest lessees of oil and gas properties, the Belzbergs held some thirty-five million acres in the late 1960s but liquidated most of them in 1969. Real estate continued to provide abundant revenues.

In 1962, Sam Belzberg launched First City Trust Company, having decided that the more established financial institutions in Toronto and Montreal didn't understand the frontier entrepreneurs of the West and would probably give them short shrift. By 1973, the Belzbergs had consolidated their real estate holdings under Western Realty Projects Ltd. Public investors owned 40 percent of the concern's stock, and the Belzbergs controlled the company with 60 percent of its outstanding shares. Deciding to cash in that year, however, the Belzbergs arranged to sell their 60 percent block to a consortium of British developers for $47.9 million. The purchase price came to $12 a share, which the family considered a fine price, particularly in light of the looming crash in real estate values both in the United States and Canada. But the Belzbergs' sellout stained the family's reputation. Left in the cold were the hapless holders of the remaining 40 percent of the stock in Western Realty Projects. They had had no opportunity to cash in on the hefty price paid by the British consortium; they had to settle for the comparatively meager market price of about $7 a share. The transaction, though legal, was considered one that most people wouldn't do.

In 1974, the family charged into California, where they acquired over 65 percent of Far West Financial Corporation. Soon after came the $41 million acquisition of Metropolitan Development Corporation, a home builder, a 49.6 percent share in Clarion Capital Corporation, a venture capital operation in Cleveland, 10 percent of Kaufman & Broad, 85 percent of Denver Real Estate Investment, and 50 percent of State Mutual Investors of Massachusetts. There were also big blocks of stock in J. Walter Thompson Company, the advertising firm; Skil Corporation, a power-tool maker, and Cordura Corporation, a direct mail marketer. By the late 1970s, the most important financial activities for the Belzberg family were coordinated under their umbrella organization, First City Financial.

The Belzbergs' attempt to acquire Bache didn't flow out of a grand scheme; at least it didn't start that way. Rather, Sam Belzberg learned to his surprise, one day in early 1979, that his family had a modest investment in Bache. An independent Toronto investment counselor reported to him that an account of idle Belzberg money had been partly invested in the shares of two Wall Street firms, Paine Webber and Bache. Belzberg's initial reaction was wariness as he recalled the Wall Street turbulence of the early seventies.

But then Belzberg began to investigate on his own. Not long after the initial purchases, he met Sandy Weill and Peter Cohen at the Regency to learn more about the business. Belzberg had carried out several real estate deals with Arthur Levitt when he was Shearson president, and respected the firm's proven ability to turn out heaping profits. Weill's and Cohen's experiences at Shearson amply demonstrated that Wall Street didn't have to be a losing business and that, in fact, it could be massively profitable. Also, it seemed to Belzberg that if First City Financial were ever to become a major purveyor of financial services, it would need some sort of distribution system. The United States–based national brokerage houses, whose stockbrokers dealt personally with investors all over the country, possessed one of the most effective distribution systems in the world. It also became clear at the meeting with Weill and Cohen that Bache was very attractive, since its stock was the greatest bargain going among the national houses. And with a profit margin lower than that of any major competitor, it stood to gain much from improved management. So Bache appealed to Belzberg's bargain-hunting instincts while offering him, theoretically at least, the prospect of making an impact on a company that appeared to be in need of strategic direction.

Sam Belzberg was an energetic man with curly golden hair and a slightly raspy voice. His manner was tough and determined, and his strong acquisitive sense lay close to the surface, lending him a restive air. His temper could be volcanic. The Bache men found Belzberg rough in manner, even rude. Jacobs told associates he was "like a truck driver."

Jacobs also stated publicly in 1979 that he had launched a search for a "suitable investor" to buy a chunk of Bache shares. The search was part of an effort to spread an effective "shark repellent" to thwart the Belzbergs and other predators. Jacobs' reference to a suitable investor also carried the disdainful message that the Belzbergs were themselves unsuitable investors, a slight that did not go unnoticed by the Canadians. Bache put forth several new rules for a shareholder vote in the fall of 1979: one proposed rule would have required a 75 percent shareholder vote, rather than a simple majority, to decide on a merger or any change in the makeup of the board. In addition, there was to be a new staggered voting system for directors so that it would take an outside group two annual shareholder meetings to gain control of the board. Further by-law changes also would have required a 75 percent shareholder vote, making it harder to undo the shark-repellent rules. And Bache proposed increasing to a million the number of shares the company could issue under an employee stock purchase plan. This would have had the effect of diluting the percentage ownership by outsiders such as the Belzbergs by pumping new shares into the hands of presumably loyal employees, who then held just over 40 percent of the outstanding Bache stock. On November 18, the rules were adopted, and Harry Jacobs was flush with relief.

Jacobs' search for a suitable investor wasn't faring so well, however. First Boston, Inc., which had brought Bache public in 1971, was scouring Europe for merchant banks that might want a toehold in the United States and was knocking on doors of big insurers that might want a stake in Wall Street. None seemed interested in the bait.

Then, in December, Harry Jacobs hopped a plane for Dallas and came up with an investor, or rather a pair of investors,

on his own. These were another set of brothers — Nelson
Bunker Hunt and William Herbert Hunt. Exactly what made
the Texas brothers suitable and the Canadian brothers unsuitable wasn't clear, except that the Texans weren't interested in taking control of the company, and the Canadians
seemed to be.

Dealing with the Hunt family represented an aberration in
the fundamentally cautious approach Bache had taken in the
securities business over the years. The Hunt relationship,
which climaxed in a near-disaster in March 1980, also seemed
out of character for Harry Jacobs. The Bache chairman was
at times a fretfully conservative man, given to looking over
traders' shoulders at the firm and instructing them to lighten
up their trading positions. And yet, even as Harry Jacobs was
praising Bache's banklike dependability in his 1979 centennial
address, the firm was extending easy credit to the Hunts in
a way that could have wiped it out before it finished its 101st
year.

One factor that may have contributed to Bache's seemingly
anomalous behavior was that the Hunts of Texas were uni-
maginably rich, richer than anyone most Wall Street financiers had ever encountered, and exponentially richer than any
of Bache's other customers, who tended to fall at the low
end of the income scale, as measured against the customers
of most big brokers. There were those at the firm who felt
the Hunts should be treated according to different standards
for this reason. Nelson Bunker Hunt, for example, was said
to have a personal net worth of $2.9 billion; his assets con-
sisted of oil and gas properties, coal properties, ranches, general real estate, cattle, racehorses, art works, rare coins, stocks,
bonds, gold, and, of course, hoards of silver. His brother
William Herbert had a personal net worth of about $1.38
billion in a comparable mixture of holdings. Nelson Bunker

(known as Bunker or Bunkie) and Herbert were the central players in Bache's tumultuous game with the billionaire dynasty. To a firm long depressed by lackluster profits, the Hunt brothers were an attractively vast source of brokerage revenue. And to a firm increasingly menaced by takeover attempts, the hugely rich brothers represented allies.

Bunker and Herbert were the fourth and fifth children of the so-called first family of Haroldson Lafayette Hunt, Jr.; their unconventional father had sired two large, separate families, more or less concurrently, in nearby homes in Dallas. In addition to the brothers' individual holdings, they held strands in a skein of Hunt interests — Placid Oil, Penrod Oil, Hunt Energy Corporation, and various partnerships in energy and commodities trading. Placid Oil Company alone produced revenues of $756 million in 1979. And when its petroleum reserves were taken into account, the energy concern had an equity value of $1.08 billion, according to a 1979 estimate by Morgan Guaranty Trust Company.

That Bache and other broker-dealers were even equipped to do commodities business with the likes of the Hunts was the result of a decade of diversification by Wall Street houses into the mysterious and sometimes treacherous game of commodities. Securities houses, adaptive organisms that they are, took to soybeans, silver, and hog bellies, in part because of the bleak level of activity in stocks during the 1970s. An executive at Shearson remarked that in 1974, with stocks cascading downward, "our managers and salesmen started to do a hell of a lot of commodities business because they wanted to eat." George D. F. Lamborn, himself from a family long involved in the sugar business, assumed the helm of Shearson's growing commodities operation, which by 1979 accounted for about 20 percent of the company's revenue.

But the commodities game could be hazardous. Futures contracts — providing for future delivery of given commodities — fluctuated daily in value. Speculators put up only a portion of the actual market value of the contracts and were regularly called on by their brokers to cough up additional margin to offset a drop in the value of the contracts in their accounts. Problems sometimes occurred for commodities brokers when customers said they weren't able to meet these margin calls, thereby putting the firms themselves on the line. For example, in 1974, when Shearson was carrying on a brisk business in sugar futures, it had a scare as a result of one such failure. The customer was an agent for the government of Costa Rica. Following a calamitous drop in the market price of sugar futures, Shearson called the man and requested additional margin. The man flatly refused, claiming that he couldn't extend any additional funds until the Costa Rican government authorized him to do so. Shearson itself then came up with $3.5 million to offset the drop in prices — no mean sum for the firm in those days. Peter Cohen, then twenty-seven, prepared to play the strongman; he was going off to Costa Rica to lay claim to a state-owned sugar plantation. But the additional margin came through, so Cohen's trip was canceled.

That incident and others led Sandy Weill to adopt a watchful attitude toward the commodities game. Said Cohen, "We started treating the commodities business like the credit business," which, indeed, it was. Each customer was examined to determine whether he was a potential credit risk to the firm. The firm also looked closely at how its customers were trading. Experience indicated that when a speculative binge got out of control, there could be problems even among the wealthiest of clients.

In 1976, the Hunts were dealing with Shearson in copper futures. With the brothers pouring millions into copper contracts each day, Weill insisted that they put up considerably more margin for their trading than they had been doing. This temporarily chilled Shearson's relationship with the Hunts, who found more sympathetic treatment at other investment houses.

Three years later, the Hunts returned to Shearson in the course of a huge buildup of futures in silver. In the summer of 1979, when silver was trading at around $10 an ounce, Weill saw to it that the Hunts were required to put up more margin.

In September, Weill and his advisers decided that, though the Hunts were meeting every margin call, their buying was out of hand. Moreover, silver prices themselves had begun fluctuating more wildly. Weill may have been Wall Street's brash entrepreneur from Brooklyn, but he had an innate caution that manifested itself when there were unusual speculative excesses. Now, he threw the Hunts out.

The Texans then found a harbor at Bache, where they had done some commodities business since 1973. Because the brothers were active traders in the silver futures, Bache understandably welcomed them. Following the practice of most firms, Bache held them to position limits, which at first kept their futures positions to forty-two hundred contracts. By 1979, the Hunts were becoming very profitable clients for Bache. In fiscal year 1978, the brothers generated $411,000 in commissions. And this preceded their aggressive buying in the silver markets.

Beginning in the fall of 1979, Bache began to alter the position limits to permit the Hunts to build up a greater futures position. The firm took in the added business from Shearson and, later, some business transferred from J. Aron & Company, a major commodities house. On October 2, Bache's commodities credit committee agreed to extend the credit line to the Hunts to seventy-five hundred contracts. The collateral was 1133 silver bullion warehouse receipts, representing 18.4 million ounces of silver, then worth about $167 million.

There was one curious aspect to the steady extension of more and more credit to the Hunts: Bache never compiled even the most basic information on how the Texas billionaires might meet cash demands. The credit file on the Hunts, in fact, was devoid of the basic data that brokers routinely gather on customers who trade on margin. The Hunts were private, sometimes eccentric people, and they responded evasively when asked by their brokers for specific financial facts. Moreover, Bache officials were so awed by the sheer magnitude of the Hunts' wealth that they shrank from pressing them for detailed financial information. Bache also refrained from inquiring about the Hunts' silver dealings at other financial houses. "It's not the type of thing you do with a customer," Fred Horn, a Bache senior vice president, later testified.

Harry Jacobs, for his part, visited the Hunts in Dallas and toured the facilities of Placid Oil and Penrod Oil. For him, these visits seemed a sufficient substitution for details of the Hunts' financial credentials. The Hunt oil concerns were obviously heavily capitalized, profitable operations. The problem, of course, was that the assets of the oil companies and of the other Hunt enterprises weren't readily available to meet credit demands arising from the Hunt brothers' silver exploits. The oil companies, for example, were controlled not by Bunker and Herbert alone, but by certain family trusts and other members of the Hunt family, too.

Bache, meanwhile, was conducting silver dealings with others in the Hunt clan. In July 1979 the firm opened a commodities futures account for Bunker's daughter Mary Hunt Huddleston, and her husband, Albert. The credit information obtained on the couple was both scanty and confusing. A letter filed in early July stated that the Huddlestons had a net worth of about $125,000 and an annual income of between $50,000 and $75,000. A letter filed several weeks later upped the net worth to $2 million and the annual income to $200,000. Both letters were kept on file. According to a Bache official

who dealt with other Hunt offspring, Bunker Hunt didn't
guarantee his children's accounts. Nevertheless, Bache increased its credit lines to the Huddlestons by a factor of 150
between July and the end of 1979. During these months, the
couple built up about $50 million in silver futures by em-
ploying a scheme whereby paper profits on existing trading
positions were used in the purchase of additional contracts.

The Hunt ties became considerably closer in late December
1979. It was then that Jacobs turned to the Texans not only
as a source of business revenue but as protection against the
takeover threat posed by the Belzbergs in Vancouver. Jacobs
flew to Dallas and asked the Hunt brothers to buy a major
block of Bache stock. They complied, purchasing 576,000
shares in Bache, or 6.67 percent of its outstanding common
stock. The Hunt investment, valued at about $5.3 million,
was a pittance to the brothers, but it would represent an
obstacle to the Belzbergs if they tried to acquire a controlling
interest in Bache. It also sent a message that Harry Jacobs
possessed powerful allies. The Hunts had pockets that were
among the deepest in the world, and if Jacobs needed further
help, the Hunts presumably could dig down even deeper and
expand their stake. Jacobs derived considerable comfort from
the brothers' agreement to buy the block of Bache shares. In
a letter he wrote the Hunts afterward he told them they had
been "a tremendous friend of Bache." And he added that
their good will "will never be forgotten, regardless of what
happens."

The crisis came during the first three months of 1980, as
Bache widened its exposure to the Hunts and their unusual
silver dealings. By the time the silver mart plunged to its
disastrous level in late March, Bache had lent $233 million
to the Hunts, an amount well over the firm's net worth.

Within a week of Harry Jacobs' trip to Dallas, Bache's

executive committee approved a doubling of the firm's loans to the Hunts, to $80 million from $40 million. These loans, which weren't actually extended until later, were to be secured by $110 million in silver warehouse receipts.

By January 1980, the financial world was buzzing with talk about the silver markets, which had taken on a frenzied, bizarre character. The price of futures contracts in silver was oscillating, and the price of silver bullion in the spot market varied as much as 9 percent from the previous day's closing. That compared with an average daily price movement of just 1.5 percent only four months earlier. The liquidity in the silver markets seemed to be drying up. An average day on the Commodity Exchange saw 7717 contracts change hands. The previous August, the average was 17,567 contracts. The talk of the unusual market behavior was filled with speculation about the Hunts; they were dominating the markets through Bache, Merrill Lynch, E. F. Hutton, and Paine Webber, to name their major Wall Street brokers. Bache held the largest share of the business. The word on the Hunts by early 1980 was that the Texas billionaires were cornering the market by building up enough of a stake to force a dramatic price movement upward.

The talk, augmented by dozens of articles in the financial press, reached a crescendo on January 7, when the Comex decided to redress things. The exchange board, empowered to exert a high degree of control over the futures markets and the way people operate in them, was determined to use its muscle. The upshot was a rule imposing new, lower position limits for all market participants. Moreover, the rule was applied retroactively, so the Hunts were going to have to lighten their existing holdings.

However, if the Hunts did much unloading, it didn't show in the marketplace. On Friday, January 17, the spot silver price surged to $50.36, up from $35.80 just ten days earlier, when the Comex had adopted the stiffer position limits. Then, on January 21, the Comex took a more drastic step. In an unusual switch, it ruled that no new orders could be placed in silver futures except to liquidate an existing position. This rule had a mighty effect: the price of silver began a two-month slide that brought it eventually to a low of $10.80 an ounce.

Amid the January turmoil, the first signs of weakness showed up in the heavily leveraged account of Albert and Mary Hunt Huddleston. The couple's futures contracts had plunged in value, and on January 24 Bache asked the Huddlestons to pay the firm the $19 million they owed in margin to offset this decline. It was an odd request to make of a couple whose annual income was either $75,000 or $200,000 and whose net worth was $125,000 or $2 million, depending on which of the two Huddleston financial statements was read. Stunned by the request, the Huddlestons informed Bache that they couldn't meet the margin call. The firm indicated it would begin liquidating the account on the following Monday. On that day the Hunt Energy Corporation wired $19 million to Bache.

Charles Mercer, an executive with Hunt Energy, was pressing Charles Mattey, a senior Bache official and a member of the firm's commodity credit committee, to secure additional loans for the Hunts. It was ultimately resolved that Bache would up its loans to the Hunts to a total of $233 million. This was secured by 2240 silver warehouse receipts that at the time well exceeded the loans in value. However, the value of the warehouse receipts was dependent on the highly volatile silver markets. And the loan was staggering when considered in the context of Bache's own financial profile: the firm's net worth came to about $154 million, as of July 1980, some $79 million less than the loan to the Hunts; its pretax earnings that year were $47.6 million, or about one-fifth the size of the Hunt loan.

The huge injection of credit came from ten big banks that lent $233 million to various Hunt interests through Bache Metals, a unit set up largely to accommodate Hunt transactions. The largest lender was First Chicago, which contributed $75 million; the other nine, which put up varying amounts, were Irving Trust, Harris Trust, Northern Trust, Bankers Trust, United States Trust, Marine Midland, First National Bank of Oklahoma City, Citizens & Southern National Bank, and Barclays International Bank.

There was considerable evidence that the Hunts could make good on the loans — although Bache didn't explore this evidence in much detail. What was at issue was the question of how quickly the billionaires could make good if they had to. The financial markets are a continuous mechanism, and the intermediaries, under the regulatory systems installed after the Great Crash, are required to respond to price movements daily, even hourly. If commodities accounts require large margin payments, the brokers carrying those accounts have to put up funds daily at the clearinghouse. Thus, the ultimate investor must be in a position to respond to calls for cash just as quickly. The Hunts, as it turned out, weren't.

By March, the liquidity in the silver markets dried up more. In mid-March, Langdon Stevenson, the Bache treasurer, had a disconcerting meeting in London with David Mann, an official of Barclays. Mann said that there was a perception in London that there simply weren't many buyers of silver, and the British banks had rebuffed the Hunts in their repeated efforts to obtain loans against silver warehouse receipts. The banks felt that the silver markets would not be able to absorb the Hunt silver put up as collateral in the event that a lender had to unload it.

Silver prices continued to slip, creating the need for additional margin in the Hunts' accounts. On March 17, Hunt Energy's Charles Mercer finally told Bache's Charles Mattey what for months the firm had assumed was an impossibility:

the Hunts couldn't pay. Stunned to learn of this, Virgil Sherrill telephoned Herbert Hunt to stress the severity of the situation. Hunt was polite. He said he and his brother understood perfectly why Bache took seriously their failure to meet their obligations. He assured the Bache president that they would do all they could to furnish the necessary cash. But he gave Sherrill no indication as to when they would do so. The billionaires were suffering a shortage of cash.

By March 19, the unrealized losses in the Hunts' futures accounts at Bache produced a margin call of $44.5 million. The amount would have been even greater but for an odd type of arithmetic used by Bache and other brokerage firms in computing margin demand. Firms figured margin by using the settlement prices in the futures markets, not in the spot markets, even though the silver bullion, if liquidated, would be sold at spot prices. In fast declines, futures prices usually sink at a slower rate than spot market prices, mainly because of trading regulations. On March 17, for example, the spot price for silver was running at about $20, $14 less than the futures price, the one used by the industry in computing margin.

Regardless of the margin arithmetic, the Hunts weren't in a position to meet Bache's demands. On March 19, the brothers said that they owned another nine million ounces of silver bullion in London, and offered to extend Bache one third of that in lieu of cash. The silver wasn't a particularly liquid asset during this period, but for the moment the Hunts still had enough around to push a portion of it at Bache to satisfy the margin call. Over the following six days, 3.6 million ounces were transferred to Bache. The remainder of the nine million, which Sherrill had demanded, wasn't.

Bache, meanwhile, reledgered the troubled Huddleston account with Bache London in order to distance the losses from the flagship brokerage unit, Bache Halsey Stuart Shields, which was subject to tight regulations governing its capital, and which was in some jeopardy of falling below the level at which the New York Stock Exchange would restrict its business activities.

Jacobs, who had been on vacation in Austria, telephoned Herbert Hunt on March 25 to demand that the brothers come up with additional cash, securities, or silver to offset the ballooning deficits in their accounts. Herbert said he would be in consultation with Bunker, who was then in Europe. Silver prices entered an even steeper slide, down from $20 an ounce. Jacobs and Sherrill then met with the Comex president Lee Berendt and other exchange officials to discuss the worsening situation. Jacobs urged the exchange to close down the markets temporarily and settle the outstanding contracts at a fixed price. The Comex executives viewed such an action as extreme and waved it down. Among other things, it would have assured the Texans a neat profit on their silver trading.

Jacobs left the meeting feeling exceedingly uneasy about the situation. That night, Herbert Hunt telephoned him at home to say that not only was there no more cash or securities to put up, but there was no more silver. Jacobs responded that this was "an extremely grave and unsatisfactory response."

The next day, Jacobs was back on the telephone to Herbert Hunt. If the Hunts couldn't pay up, Bache would be forced to start liquidating the brothers' accounts at whatever prices their contracts and bullion would bring. Herbert said the firm should do whatever it needed to do. As Jacobs was directing the appropriate officials at Bache to dispatch telegrams to various Hunt family members, stating that Bache would begin liquidating the silver accounts, Bunker Hunt made a startling announcement in Paris. On Wednesday morning, March 26, he stated that he and four Arab partners had acquired more than two hundred million ounces of silver and that the group planned to issue silver bonds backed by the metal. If the plan had worked — which it didn't — Hunt would have created one of the strongest currencies in the world.

That diversion did nothing to lessen the Hunts' cash squeeze, which was making Bache's own needs more acute. The firm had been forced to cough up $22 million a day at the Comex clearinghouses to satisfy margin demands arising from deficits in the Hunt accounts. It was industry practice for the clearinghouses to charge the firms each day, then leave it to the firms to collect the necessary funds from their individual customers. By March 26, Bache had paid $156 million to the clearinghouses without collecting a sou from the Hunts. With silver prices falling inexorably, the continuing cash drain looked grave. Bache began selling the silver bullion the Hunts had put up as collateral, but they did so at slumping prices.

At twelve-fifteen on the 26th, Jacobs telephoned Federal Reserve Board chairman Paul Volcker. The call had two purposes: Jacobs wanted to inform the nation's central banker of the worsening problem and get whatever support he could; Jacobs also wanted Volcker to pressure the Comex to shut down trading, as he had unsuccessfully urged the exchange to do the previous day. The alternative solution would be for the Comex to lighten the margin requirements, thus staunching the cash drain Bache was suffering daily.

On that Wednesday afternoon, the Comex Board of Governors met in emergency session. Jacobs and Sherrill were huddled anxiously outside the board room. The board rejected Jacobs' proposal that it close trading, but it did go along with Jacobs' other suggestion, that margin requirements be lightened to lessen the cash drain on Bache. Meanwhile, silver's slide downward continued relentlessly, finishing the day at $15.80, down $4.40 from the previous day's close.

That evening, Jacobs and Sherrill convened at the Drake Hotel in New York with Herbert Hunt and the other Hunt brokers. The meeting was chaotic, and tensions ran high. The Hunts' cash shortage hadn't changed since Jacobs' conversation with Herbert that morning.

Thursday, March 27, brought a rising sense of panic. The day was later dubbed Silver Thursday, a reference to Black Thursday of 1929. With silver prices plunging, and the Hunts unable to pay Bache what they owed it, the firm was in a potentially fatal position. The Securities and Exchange Commission saw enough of the problem to insist that trading in Bache shares be halted until April 5, or as soon as the mess had resolved itself.

Rumors of crisis were traveling throughout the financial world. In the money business, perceptions of financial trouble can be as perilous as failure itself. If an organization is believed to be in jeopardy, other participants recoil in an effort to protect their own assets, and it soon finds itself cut off from the funds and business it needs to remain afloat. So it was with Bache on Silver Thursday. First, the ten banks whose loans had supported the $233 million extension of credit to the Hunts were becoming nervous. But there was another tier of jittery bankers who had supplied Bache with the funds for conducting its day-to-day operations. Two of the banks that had been helping Bache meet the $22 million-a-day margin calls at the exchange clearinghouse — Credit Italiano and Crédit Lyonnais — cut off further loans and demanded repayment of what they had lent. The Chicago Board of Trade clearinghouse demanded $20 million in margin.

Within the securities business itself, firms and institutions began dealing with Bache in a gingerly way. Financial houses hesitated to supply Bache with securities it bought unless the firm put up cash. Traders on the commodities exchange had heard that the Hunts or the Hunts' brokers would be unloading great amounts of both silver futures and silver bullion to raise cash. Given the downward pressure this selling would exert on the markets, others decided to unload their own holdings before things got worse. The stampede of sellers naturally exacerbated an already catastrophic price decline. The frenzy spread to the stock market, as well. There, word had it that the Hunts or their brokers would be dumping big blocks from the family stock portfolio, which included large investments in Gulf Resources & Chemical.

The family also did business with Merrill Lynch, which carried the accounts of the International Metals Investments Company, a Bermuda concern jointly owned by the Hunts and two Saudi businessmen, Ali Bin Mussalam and Mohammed Abou Al-Amoudi. The Texans were also sending shudders through the other houses where there were Hunt accounts, but none of these firms had the exposure that Bache did.

New York Stock Exchange examiners arrived to pore over Bache's books on Thursday morning. About midday, Nelson Kibler, a top SEC official, telephoned Shearson's Peter Cohen. "We don't know whether it's going to be necessary," he said, "but how many Bache offices could you take on if you had to?"

Cohen was shocked to learn that the predicament was this bad. "Oh, shit. I'll call you back," he said. After huddling with Sandy Weill, he dialed Kibler back to say Shearson could take on thirty or forty if it had to. Kibler was calling around to others, too.

The Hunts' brokers were unloading silver and silver futures at whatever prices they would bring. E. F. Hutton dumped a hoard of silver bullion supporting a $100 million loan it had extended to the Hunts. Bache had sold 7.75 million ounces of silver the previous day and on Thursday was selling more silver bullion and silver futures from the brokers' accounts. One item that wasn't to be liquidated during the emergency rush to the markets was the 576,000-share block of Bache stock, bought at Jacobs' request as an obstacle to the Belz-bergs. In the thick of the crisis, Jacobs had left instructions that this investment be left intact.

At about 2:00 P.M. on March 27, silver hit a low of $10.80 an ounce on the spot market; it had traded at $20.20 just two days earlier and at $50.35 on January 17. Things were equally grisly in the stock market. The bellwether Dow Jones Industrial Average had plunged 26 points by this time. Peter Cohen stepped into Weill's office with an expression of horror on his face. "This thing is out of control," he said. The two men went to the kitchen of the Shearson headquarters, where Cohen poured himself a tumbler of Scotch and prepared an equally bracing drink of gin for Weill. However prudently Shearson handled the Hunts, it would be affected if a firm as large as Bache went under because of the Hunts' cash shortage. No one could be sure just how far the shock waves would travel. What if there were bank failures? What if other securities houses were brought down in the process? One of them, Paine Webber — in the throes of a crippling back-office crisis arising from its inability to absorb efficiently the business of Blyth Eastman Dillon, which it had just acquired — could be sent over the brink.

By three o'clock, the Dow Jones had sunk 32 points. Then something happened. The sense of doom seemed to have lifted, at least in the stock market. The investing institutions, seeing cheap stocks available, started buying in droves. As prices spurted upward, more institutions jumped in, and by the four o'clock close the market was up, only 2.14 points lower than the previous day's close.

The happy reversal on the Stock Exchange by no means resolved the pending disaster at Bache. In Washington, there was a top-level silver watch, consisting of Volcker, the SEC's Harold Williams, James Stone, chairman of the Commodity Futures Trading Commission, and Deputy Secretary of the

Treasury Robert Carswell. The four men monitored the situation throughout the day.

At five o'clock, the New York Stock Exchange member firms' surveillance committee convened for an emergency meeting. Jacobs and Sherrill arrived shortly afterward. Bache had by this time sold off fifteen million ounces of the Hunts' silver bullion, and about twice that amount still remained in the family accounts at Bache. Bache's capital position had deteriorated. Under the New York Stock Exchange rule 325(b), a member firm's capital can't fall below 7 percent of its aggregate indebtedness from customer transactions without triggering an early-warning mechanism. This throws the firm under moment-by-moment surveillance by the Exchange and brings a prohibition against further extensions of customer debt. Bache, which had been running capital of about $70 million in excess of the warning level, was in danger of slipping below the threshold. The extra capital could be wiped out by yet another unmet margin call arising from further drops in the price of silver. It was determined that if the price of silver, which had slipped almost $10 in the previous two days, descended another $2.80 per ounce, Bache would fall beneath the 7 percent threshold. Despite the precarious situation, Jacobs and Sherrill urged the Exchange to shore up the firm's reputation by issuing a news release stating that Bache was in compliance with all applicable capital regulations and that Bache shares would soon resume trading. The Exchange sternly refused to issue any such statement.

As dusk settled, and the sidewalks of Wall Street grew desolate, a parade of limousines pulled up to the Exchange edifice at 11 Wall, delivering various potentates of finance. It was to be a long, troubled night at the Big Board. In other financial centers, things weren't much different. Financial leaders throughout the world hung anxiously on each word about what was happening and what was yet to happen.

Between dusk and midnight, something did happen. Whether it was an arranged form of support for the silver markets or simply an alchemical change in the market has been the subject of subsequent speculation, but something occurred to halt the thundering approach of a crisis. At twelve-thirty that night, Peter Cohen telephoned Edmond Safra, the chief of the Geneva-based Trade Development Bank, a very successful international bank that controlled Republic National Bank of New York, where Cohen had worked in 1978. Safra was one of the world's richest and, by reputation, one of its most brilliant bankers. The Lebanese-born financier was no speculator himself, but he would be profoundly affected by a crisis in the silver markets, because he operated as an intermediary in the precious metals dealings of hundreds of wealthy clients. Cohen's twelve-thirty call was perhaps the twentieth conversation the two men had had on Silver Thursday. (It was Friday morning in Geneva.) The previous Safra-Cohen conversations on that day had been charged with enormous worry, but this talk was mysteriously different; there was a sense of calm. "Don't worry," the banker said; "silver won't trade below eleven dollars. I have orders to buy three million ounces of silver, and I'm just one of the players."

Safra's prophecy was accurate. On the London Metal Exchange, which opens five hours earlier than the United States' marts and which generally determines prices for trading worldwide, silver began trading at $11 and then bounced about at prices ranging up to $15 an ounce. The worst of the storm had passed. Volcker and the other watchmen in Washington concluded that, with prices holding at about $11, there was no reason to consider such emergency measures as shutting down trading.

Some financial executives felt that Volcker himself had quietly arranged for the market support that brought the prices up. Others speculated that Bunker Hunt, who was then meeting with business partners in Saudi Arabia, had orchestrated the turnaround. Others, probably with greater accuracy, reasoned that silver had reached a point at which the managers of big pools of money considered it an excellent buy. It is, after all, at those times when most of the world is quaking with fear and suspicion that the proverbial "smart money" pours in.

The market crisis having been averted, Bache was faced with straightening up a disordered state of affairs internally and repairing a ravaged image. The first order of business on Friday morning was a meeting with the ten banks that had supplied the capital used to make the $233 million loans to the Hunts. Bache officials ran through detailed reports of how much silver and how many futures had been sold and at what prices. Data were also provided on the capital position of the firm. Bache was eager to restore confidence in its operation and to start the trading again in Bache shares. On Friday afternoon, the firm got the banks to give their blessing to a release stating that Bache had liquidated all the Hunt positions with no loss to the firm, that Bache was in full compliance with all applicable capital regulations, and that the subordinated lenders had made $24 million available for any problems that might arise. It was a forceful-sounding release aimed at disspelling the grave doubts that had debilitated the firm. The release was also untrue.

As Bache officials discovered over the weekend, on a more methodical inspection of the books, the liquidation of the Hunt account had produced $10 million in deficits. Moreover, there were 6.9 million ounces of silver bullion left on the books, and, at spot prices, these would bring a sum that was $22 million less than what Bache still owed the ten banks. There was also the nagging matter of Mary and Albert Huddleston's account, temporarily shuffled out of sight via the reledgering to Bache London. Although the Huddlestons had been overlooked on Friday, their account had been liquidated at a deficit of $23 million.

On Monday, March 31, the firm issued another news release, in which it conceded that there were, in fact, $10 million in losses in the liquidated Hunt accounts at Bache Halsey, these being partly secured by the unshakable block of Bache stock that the Hunts had bought at Jacobs' behest three months earlier. The release also stated that there might be about $40 million in potential losses from Hunt family accounts kept at Bache Metals and Bache London. Bache's bankers were irate at the change in news. But Monday also brought relief — the long-awaited first payment from the Hunts. The brothers had by this time worked out a complex arrangement with Placid Oil, whereby considerable amounts of cash were unleashed. The sum of $17 million was delivered to Bache at once. Other payments followed over the ensuing weeks, and the Texans' obligations were eventually honored in full.

In April, Bache wrote to all its customers, and took out an ad in the newspapers, stating that Bache's clients hadn't been harmed by the silver crisis (they hadn't), that Bache had met all its obligations to the clearinghouses and other market participants, and that "at no time did these events require Bache to seek additional capital by borrowing or any other means. Not one penny." Neither the customer letter nor the ad, which was titled "A Test of Strength," mentioned that to accomplish these results Bache had had to reledger the Huddleston accounts to London and obtain from the Comex reduced margin requirements.

Some eighteen months later, the New York Stock Exchange fined Bache $400,000 for its performance in the silver crisis, the largest fine ever imposed by the Big Board on a member firm. "The firm permitted certain of its customers to maintain quantities of futures contracts on margin which were of such magnitude that they created the potential for a material adverse impact on the firm's financial condition," the Exchange said. The Big Board also criticized Bache for issuing confusing and contradictory reports on what was happening during the mess.

The silver crisis seemed to etch permanently Bache's image as a bungler. Brokers, who had to deal with customers, were exhausted from proffering explanations that the firm, and its customers' assets, were safe. Some brokers, having had enough, took off for other firms.

One of the vocal Wall Street critics of Bache's handling of the silver mess was Sandy Weill. When word traveled back to Jacobs that Weill was taking shots at Bache, the defensive Bache chairman telephoned the Shearson chief to express his dismay. Weill, surprised by the call, was nonetheless blunt in his response to it. "You nearly set us back ten years," he told Jacobs. "I don't know what you're focusing on."

Andrew Racz, a securities analyst, moved in quick, excited steps around an ill-lit office in one of a pair of Gothic buildings rising from the north end of the Trinity Church graveyard. In the fall of 1980, he was bubbling over with excitement about the implications of Ronald Reagan's expected election, of billion-dollar financings expected in the energy and industrial areas, and of a generally improved investment climate. It all appeared to spell lavish profits for the Wall Street houses. As Racz saw it, the gambling industry stocks had had their day in the late 1970s, the energy stocks were still riding the crest, and now the stocks of Wall Street firms were about to have their moment. Securities houses were the prosperity merchants. They had weathered the turmoil, Racz believed, and the unvanquished stood poised to inherit the bounty of the 1980s. Racz had a special role to play in shaping the future of the financial world, but this hadn't yet been defined.

Racz, Hungarian-born, was short, round, and furry-looking, with a bushy mass of dark brown hair and a scurrying way of walking. His gray eyes were almost always opened wide, and he generally toted a hefty cigar, which, though out of scale with his small frame and tiny, plump hands, lent him the air of a 1930s-style financier. Racz operated autonomously within Philips, Appel & Walden, grandly dubbing his arm of the company Racz International. He usually spoke in a soft, excited patter clothed in an Eastern European accent. He spent much of his day on the telephone, conducting each conversation with the sort of breathless urgency that suggested that the stock market was either about to crash or to soar to new heights. He would end conversations abruptly, uttering the word "Pleasure" into the phone and laying down the receiver.

Racz employed his own brand of securities analysis. In contrast to the gray mathematical reports turned out by some of the big financial factories, Racz's research reports were attractively packaged in individual cream-colored booklets, some containing photographs of the interview subjects or reproductions of etchings of old Wall Street. These reports consisted of long, transcribed interviews with the chief executives of the companies; they also contained florid, self-dramatizing passages of Racz's own analogies and reminiscences.

Racz was an unapologetic opportunist. "I create interest in stocks," he once said, flashing an impish grin. He then moved on to discuss the latest company whose stock he had favored with a research report.

In August 1980, Andrew Racz composed what was his most dramatic, and most peculiar, research report — on Bache Group, Inc. Racz enjoyed evoking great figures of history in his executive interviews, and in the report on Bache, he chose Winston Churchill. According to Racz, Bache's role in the Hunt silver debacle had been one of heroism — previously unremarked. The cover of the report carried some earnings information on the firm, under which, in bold type, was the Churchill quotation "This was their finest hour!!"

Throughout, Racz lavishly praised Bache and its management for selling out the Hunts' silver bullion after being informed that the Texas billionaires didn't have the cash to meet the firm's margin calls. "You had the power, the capital, and the decisiveness to act in what I may call your finest hour," Racz gushed. Nowhere, however, did the report take up the more pressing question of exactly why Bache had so extended itself to the Hunts in the first place. Instead, there were assertions that the major securities houses were on the brink of a hugely profitable era. Presumably, Bache would share in it.

To help stir up as much activity as possible in Bache shares, Racz began mapping plans for a reception at which he would unveil the unusual report. Money managers from the major banks and pension funds would be invited, along with other Wall Street dignitaries, such as William M. Batten, the Stock Exchange chairman. Bache, which was already embarrassed by the report's odd interpretation of the silver mess, discouraged the notion of a ceremony. Racz then took out advertisements in *Barron's* to announce the Bache report. The ads carried a picture of the report, complete with the quotation from Churchill.

The contretemps over the reception, and Jacobs' negative reaction to the fawning research report, were the beginning of a chill between Racz and the Bache chief. But some of Racz's institutional clients began buying shares in Bache, providing a modest flow of commissions for him.

Not long after the report came out, Racz went to the Regency for dinner with his fiancée. It was a location where he could be assured of an encounter with one or more corporate moguls who used the sumptuous hotel as a New York headquarters. By coincidence, Racz ran into the one executive he was most eager to huddle with — Sam Belzberg. Racz had telephoned Belzberg after publishing his Bache report. "You are in Bache. I am in Bache. Let's get to know each other," Racz said. During the chance encounter at the Regency, the two agreed to talk the following day. When they met, it became clear that they might be able to do business. Specifically, Racz told Belzberg that he had gotten to know the Hunt brothers in 1975, when he had tried to sell them an energy concern. Since he had remained in contact with them, he might be able to shake loose the block of Bache stock held by the Hunts and move at least some of it into the hands of the Belzbergs. Such a transaction, of course, would spectacularly foil Bache's underlying purpose in placing the shares with the Hunt brothers — as protection against the Belzberg brothers. Sam Belzberg urged Racz to proceed with the negotiations with the Hunts. There would be a handsome commission if Racz pulled it off.

By September, Racz was able to arrange a breakfast meeting with Bunker Hunt at the Carlyle Hotel. Racz had brought along his eleven-year-old son from his previous marriage, believing it would be an exciting experience for the boy to breakfast with a billionaire. The conversation was fairly brief. Following the silver fiasco, Hunt felt no loyalty toward Bache nor any obligation to protect the firm from predators by holding on to his Bache shares. When Racz explained that he could liquidate the Hunts' holdings in Bache at a good price, Hunt was clearly receptive. Few questions were asked about just who would be buying the shares, although anyone following the action in Bache's stock would have logically assumed that the Belzberg brothers would be bidding. It was a short breakfast. "You can't talk with Hunt a long time," Racz said. But by the time he left the Carlyle with his son, he knew he had a deal.

As it turned out, about half of the Hunts' holdings — or 317,130 shares — went to the Belzbergs, bringing their stake in Bache to 13.96 percent of its outstanding stock. The other portion of the Hunt block went to Stanley Mann, a wealthy and intensely private chief executive of Diamond Industries, a closely held business he had inherited from his father sixteen years earlier. Mann, who ended up bankrolling certain ventures for Racz, was the sort of person Racz was drawn to. He was aloof and mysterious. He owned houses in Philadelphia and Palm Beach and continuously made quiet deals that nourished his portfolio significantly without creating much stir. Racz, who was hardly inconspicuous, admired men who operated less noticeably than he did.

The reshuffling of the Hunt block and the subsequent purchases in Bache stock produced groans at Bache. Jacobs, Racz later said, "was more frightened of Mann than of the Belzbergs." It did seem that the Mann stake — about 3.3 percent of Bache's common — introduced a new player into the Byzantine struggle for the company's shares. Jacobs, however, insisted that Mann's investment never became an important factor and dismissed Racz's assertion to the contrary as drivel.

The successful peddling of the Hunt block of Bache shares was a source of enormous pride to Racz, who savored the idea of operating among the most powerful and famous financial powers. "I write a report, and then I want to take the maximum revenue-producing posture," he said after the transactions. "These trades have not made me a rich man," he said. But, then, his concept of a rich man had undoubtedly been altered by his traffic with the Hunts and the Belzbergs.

Andrew Racz had succeeded in becoming a self-appointed auctioneer in Bache's stock, moving multimillion-dollar blocks of it from one big-dollar investor to another. And as a result of his new role, the analyst began getting calls from Harry Jacobs when the transaction tape showed that Bache shares were changing hands in large amounts. Racz, meanwhile, had concluded that Jacobs was bad-mouthing him and had even set off the investigation of his research and deal-making by the Federation of Financial Analysts, a probe that was later dropped without any action. As a result of the growing resentments and suspicions, the conversations between Jacobs and Racz became more tense.

As Racz's relationship with Jacobs deteriorated, the analyst's ties with the Belzbergs grew cozier. On November 8, 1980, Racz was married, and after a reception at the Tavern on the Green in Central Park, he flew to Los Angeles with his bride. The following day, the Raczes attended a party at Bill Belzberg's home in Beverly Hills. The Belzberg family was in town in connection with a fund-raising effort for the Simon Wiesenthal Center for Holocaust Studies, to which the Belzbergs were large contributors.

At the party, Racz cornered Sam Belzberg. "The brokerage business is going to boom — nineteen eighty-one is going to be the year," Racz said in his most intense whisper. "Go ahead." Racz had no specific suggestions, but he felt the Belzbergs should become more openly aggressive, perhaps by making a tender offer for the Bache shares they didn't already own, or by staging a proxy fight to topple Jacobs and Sherrill.

But Sam Belzberg was hesitant. He remained hopeful that he could be viewed as a friendly investor in Bache, that he could gain a position on the board of the firm and become involved in its business affairs. He believed that Harry Jacobs' passionate and visceral opposition to the family was no more than a communication problem that could be corrected through businesslike discussion. Belzberg was resolved to have one more face-to-face meeting with the Bache chairman.

On December 16, 1980, Jacobs met Sam Belzberg, alone, at four o'clock at the American Airlines Admiral Club at

LaGuardia Airport. Belzberg, who had set up the meeting, tried to open the session on friendly terms, saying he felt that his and Jacobs' relationship had gotten off to a poor start because the two chief executives were always surrounded by a retinue of lawyers and aides. He also repeated that it was his overriding desire to gain some representation on Bache's board. Belzberg even said that he would have halted the buying of Bache shares long ago, when the family owned only 5 percent, if he had been given a seat on the board. Jacobs sat stiff and unyielding.

According to notes Jacobs penned as he was chauffeured home after the strained meeting, Belzberg had become more and more aggressive. "As the meeting wore on, the cordiality dimmed," Jacobs wrote, and Belzberg pushed harder for one or two board seats. Jacobs' recorded account of the meeting suggests that Belzberg was alternately pleading and threatening. Summarizing the Canadian's words, Jacobs wrote: " 'I will bring a lot to the party. I can help the firm. My lawyers told me I could cause a lot of trouble at the annual meeting but I decided not to.' "

Belzberg also told Jacobs that if the firm was not going to offer him a place on its board, he was " 'going to make a move within the next year,' " according to the memo. "He's got a foreign group that wants to buy 20–25% of the company. They have the management."

Jacobs ended his memo with the following prediction: "They will own 40–45% of the company and everybody else will be starved out."

It was necessary, under Bache's corporate charter, that Jacobs submit Sam Belzberg's proposal to the company's nominating committee for consideration. This was a five-member group that included Jacobs and Sherrill. Its attitude toward the Belzberg matter flowed from its fundamental support of Harry Jacobs' chairmanship, for the fifty-nine-year-old chairman was so adamant in his determination to fend off the Canadians that to oppose him on this issue was tantamount to challenging his leadership. Also, it was generally believed that if Belzberg ever attained a seat on the firm's board, Jacobs would have to resign.

After the nominating committee ratified Jacobs' stand, the Bache chief began to devise a means of communicating the decision to the Belzbergs. He concluded that Clark Clifford, the former Cabinet member and presidential adviser, should speak for the firm on the matter. Clifford, who had been brought on as a Washington counsel by Harold Bache in the 1960s and drew on an authority that lay outside the firm itself, could tell the Canadians that they would be unsuitable board members. Coming from Clark Clifford, the message would somehow seem to be an edict from the United States.

Clifford agreed to play emissary and summoned Sam Belzberg to Washington to discuss the matter. The struggle was near its dénouement, and there was neither room nor necessity for tact. Bache was ready to reveal the extent to which it had been "checking" on the Belzbergs, a charge Sam Belzberg had leveled at the LaGuardia meeting. Clifford confronted Belzberg with a sheaf of paper related to the family's several business activities. Jacobs and others at Bache were worried that the family might have ties to the Mafia, he said. The concern stemmed from the discovery — in the course of what began as "due diligence" but grew into global detective work by Bache — of a peculiar incident that had taken place eleven years earlier in Acapulco. In February 1970, dozens of alleged Mafia leaders from the United States and Canada assembled at the Acapulco Hilton to sift plans for infiltrating the casino business they correctly expected to mushroom in the years ahead at Atlantic City. The meeting was considered by law enforcement officials to be the largest such convocation since 1957, when gangland leaders met in Appalachin,

New York. At the center of the Acapulco session was Meyer Lansky, considered the financial wizard of the crime syndicate and one of the kingpins of the underworld.

Law enforcers were following Lansky's movements extremely closely by 1970, and the Acapulco area was brimming with agents of the Federal Bureau of Investigation, the U.S. Treasury Department's Bureau of Customs, and the Royal Canadian Mounted Police. A report prepared by the Bureau of Customs after the meeting noted that "a Mr. and Mrs. H. Belzberg of Calgary, Alberta," were at the Acapulco Hilton at the time. The report also stated that the Belzbergs "were frequently seen with Lansky," along with Benny Kaufman, a Lansky intimate from Montreal. The report did not say that Belzberg attended meetings held by Lansky or other mob leaders at the time.

On the basis of the evidence on file, Bache executives believed they had ample justification for opposing the Belzbergs. At the same time, Clifford suggested that, in light of the information Bache had gathered, the Belzbergs should retreat to avoid any airing of Bache's concerns.

The message, though it was delivered by one of the most powerful figures of twentieth-century American politics, had the opposite effect from what it was intended to have. Sam Belzberg was enraged; he felt that Clifford's message was blackmail and that Bache's defense against takeover had descended to the level of smear tactics. Now there was no turning back for Belzberg.

By this time, there was the overarching matter of family pride. In the wake of the insult, Sam Belzberg, who usually was motivated by economic considerations, "was reacting emotionally," an associate said, adding that the Clifford message had had the effect of "lighting a fuse."

The purchases of Bache shares picked up steam. On January 14, the Belzbergs snapped up fifteen thousand shares. On the following day, they bought another seventy-one hundred. Through purchases made on January 23, 28, and 29, and February 3 and 9, the brothers raked in an additional 223,800 shares, which brought their stake to 21.1 percent. Sam Belzberg was meeting constantly with Joe Flom and his colleague Robert Pirie at Skadden Arps and with other friends and advisers in New York. Gershon Kekst, a public relations man who was often enlisted in merger wars, advised Belzberg to end a strictly observed silence with the New York press and to meet with certain reporters before the Bache struggle intensified further. In the subsequent interviews, Belzberg would emphasize his family's philanthropic activities — its large gifts to the Simon Wiesenthal Center and its generous support for medical research on dystonia, a rare neurological disease his daughter had suffered from. Then his knuckles would whiten, and he would insist that he wasn't backing down, regardless of the position Jacobs had taken.

The Mafia matter stemmed from "an absolute coincidence," Belzberg insisted. Benny Kaufman operated a rug dealership in Montreal, among other things, and for some years had known Hyman, who ran the Belzberg furniture concern. The Canadian Mounties had independently investigated all Canadian guests at the Hilton who might have links to Lansky and had taken no steps against Hyman Belzberg.

Friends of the Belzberg family depicted the eldest brother as being a personable though bumbling sort of man who seemed to gravitate toward awkward predicaments. "It's been the joke of the family for years," said a partner from Salomon Brothers. "Only Hymie could end up on the beach with these people and not know who they are."

Acting on the assumption that he might someday be in a position to dislodge Jacobs and Sherrill, Sam Belzberg began combing the financial world for managers he could bring in to displace them. Belzberg called Peter Cohen to see whether he could wrest him from Shearson. Another call went to Arthur Carter, of the original Carter, Berlind, Potoma & Weill. Top officials at Bache began to consider it likely that the Belzbergs would eventually gain control of the company.

Active in its own defense, a core group of Bache officials — Jacobs, Sherrill, John Curran, the general counsel, and Delayne Gold, the public relations vice president — convened each morning at eight-thirty to review the latest moves by the Belzbergs and to discuss the tactics open to Bache. Jacobs, according to one adviser, was "obsessed" with the Belzbergs and focused on little else. Occasionally, he would refer to the predictions he had scrawled in his pocket notebook — that the Belzbergs would seek to control the company and would then unseat its management.

The firm was working to gain more information on the possible Mafia link suggested by the Acapulco report. Bache hired an investigator in Israel to research an unverified report that Sam Belzberg had intervened on behalf of Meyer Lansky when the underworld figure sought asylum in Israel to escape federal indictments in the United States. The Israeli government, which ultimately denied Lansky a haven, refused to discuss the matter with Bache's emissary. The firm also had a detective working in Canada. There was one report that the Mounties had destroyed a file of information on the Belzbergs, after which a truckload of furniture from Hyman's emporium was delivered to the official responsible. The Mounties steadfastly denied this report.

While Bache was carrying out its research, it was also accelerating a program of buying up insurance agencies. Since Bache bought the agencies by issuing its own shares, the acquisitions had the effect of diluting the stake owned by the Belzbergs. In addition, Bache bought a Las Vegas municipal bond house and a smelting company to work alongside its precious metals' unit. The firm also began exploring the purchase of a savings and loan institution, which would have brought Bache under the purview of the Federal Home Loan Bank Board and might have involved the Belzbergs in new regulatory red tape.

By March, the Belzbergs held close to 25 percent of the outstanding shares in Bache. Jacobs seemed to be losing ground. Bache's small-time acquisitions diluted the Belzbergs' stake only momentarily until the brothers could buy up another mound of shares. On March 2, Jacobs called over Robert Bayliss, a First Boston investment banker who had worked with Bache since its initial public offering in 1971. Then Jacobs made the first effective defense against the Belzbergs since they had started their purchases two years earlier. He put his company up for sale. The choice was an agonizing one, but as Jacobs saw it, there wasn't much else he could do. He faced the choice of harboring the old firm in some respectable, vastly capitalized financial company or watching it fall prey to intruders from Canada. Thus it was that Bache found its way to the auction block.

First Boston, as it happened, had become one of the most aggressive takeover experts on Wall Street. The firm had helped Pullman, Inc., stave off MacDermott, Inc., in 1980, and had counseled St. Joe Minerals in repulsing Canada's Seagram Distillers, owned by the Bronfmans, another family bent on spreading its southward expansion. First Boston's merger team — headed by Joseph R. Perella and Bruce Wasserstein — managed to generate some $75 million in merger fees in 1981.

The First Boston merger people were the prototypes of the newest breed on Wall Street. These were the merger barons — the fee-hungry takeover specialists who fed on American companies' passion for combining. They were young, often from Harvard and Stanford business schools. They lived for making the deals that produced heaping fees for their firms and, through incentive bonus systems, made them millionaires in their thirties. Most of the takeover people were predictably garbed in the three-piece suits their superiors wore. But they were inherently different, for the new breed was part of the "me generation" and had gone through the period of self-absorption before hitting the lucrative world of finance. Their egos required the satisfaction of selling or buying companies valued in the hundreds of millions or billions. Few of the merger-makers were concerned about whether the combinations they had engineered ever worked out, let alone whether the huge expense of energy and money devoted to takeovers was productive. They were simply in business "to do deals," as the vernacular had it, and to initiate them when they didn't materialize on their own.

Companies moved fast once the merger people brought them into play. As First Boston was drawing up a list of white knights to rescue Bache from the Belzbergs, others caught sight of the willing takeover target. Among them was Morgan Stanley's Robert Greenhill, one of Wall Street's takeover experts, notorious for his brash ways and his suspenders embroidered with gold dollar signs. Greenhill quickly found a potential buyer in Beneficial Financial Corporation, the big consumer finance company, and insisted on negotiations one weekend at Sullivan & Cromwell. The talks fizzled, and the matter was again in the hands of the First Boston merger team.

Other prospective acquirers included Baldwin-United, the old Cleveland piano-maker, which was pushing its way into financial services, and Transamerica Corporation. Then Bayliss informed Jacobs that there had also been a nibble of interest from the giant Prudential Insurance Corporation of America. Jacobs assumed at first that since Prudential was a mutual company — owned by its policyholders — the purchase of a publicly owned securities firm would not be possible. Nevertheless, he and Sherrill met with Frank Hoenemeyer, the top investment executive at Prudential, and David Sherwood, a high-ranking strategist with the company. It turned out that Prudential, which had some $62 billion in assets, had been studying its own future and had concluded that diversification into new investment-type activities would be profitable. The Pru had targeted mutual funds, among other things, as an attractive sideline. The company also wanted to upgrade its customer base. Bache, though at the low end of major securities firms, had customers with average annual incomes of $40,000, which was more than $15,000 higher than the corresponding average for Prudential customers. And as to mutual funds, Bache had built up a family of them.

Then, too, the investment business was hardly new to Prudential. It managed billions in pension assets and invested the waves of money that flowed in through its own insurance activities. Pru Capital, a subsidiary, operated like a commercial bank, selling commercial paper — or short-term IOUs — then lending money at short-term floating rates to small- or medium-size companies. Prudential was a large factor in real estate markets and in leasing activities.

Buying a securities house seemed to be a logical move, given the direction in which the company was going. It might also correct a problem that had cropped up in recent years: life insurance policyholders were borrowing money against their policies at the giveaway rate of 5 percent. Since Prudential and other insurers were borrowing at 15 to 20 percent, the outflow was costly. Prudential officials reasoned that, because some of this money was flowing into high-yielding money market funds, a securities firm could recapture what was leaving.

On March 19, Prudential's top executives arrived at Sullivan & Cromwell with a full retinue of lawyers and accountants. They were ready to name a price. It was decided that the insurer would pay $32 a share, or a total price of $385 million for Bache. This amount equaled the Pru's cash flow over a period of about three weeks.

Danny Pekarsky, one of Sam Belzberg's closest aides in Vancouver, heard of the merger talks and left a message at the Edmonton airport for his boss to telephone him when he touched down there en route to London. Belzberg called, and Pekarsky told him he had heard Bache was about to be bought for $40 a share.

The price, announced the following morning, was considerably lower, of course. The Prudential merger was a deep disappointment to Belzberg. "It was a denial of his opportunity to try his talents in the largest marketplace in the world," Pekarsky said. Nevertheless, when the Belzberg camp combed through its ledger book, it saw that the family would realize a profit of about $40 million on the sale of its Bache shares.

Sandy Weill learned of the Prudential bid on the morning of March 20, through a brief news article run in the *South China Morning Post,* which arrived at his suite at the Mandarin Hotel in Hong Kong. Weill was there with Gerald Ford, a Shearson board member, to visit the firm's highly profitable Hong Kong office. Joan Weill, not knowing what he was reading, watched her husband's face lock in an expression that was both quizzical and alarmed. She sensed that something was going to happen.

Weill knew that the competitive balance on Wall Street had been changed inalterably. Bache had never posed much of a competitive threat for Weill, whose firm was the second largest in the business and the most profitable of any publicly owned brokerage house. But now Bache was to be owned by one of the world's biggest financial institutions, with more than $60 billion in total assets. Knowing Wall Street's lemming instincts, Weill felt sure that other firms would sell out, either to big insurance companies like Prudential or to some other corporate entities that would give them the means to compete in the world of financial services' superpowers. It seemed that Sandy Lewis' prophecies at the breakfast the previous August were proving to be correct. One wouldn't talk about just the brokerage business any longer; now it would be the money business. A company could combine nearly all aspects of finance.

Back in New York, Jim Robinson was having similar thoughts. Predictably, Lewis telephoned Robinson at six forty-five in the morning, just after seeing the paper. "Well," the American Express chief said in his Georgia drawl, "it's a whole new ball game." Robinson asked whether Lewis thought Weill was still interested in merging. "This guy is as honest as the day is long," Lewis said. "He's told you he's interested in something like this, and if this thing is the catalyst, so be it." He told Robinson that he'd get to work setting up a meeting with Weill.

After he hung up, Lewis paused for a moment. "Thank you, Mr. Belzberg," he said aloud. "I've never met you, but thank you." Then he telephoned Weill's office to try to track down the Shearson chief. After telling Weill's secretary that he had to speak to her boss on a life-or-death matter, he got the telephone number at the Mandarin. That night he called Hong Kong and reached Weill in the hotel.

"It appears to me that Jim is of a mind to go ahead," he said. "Where are you?"

"I think I'd like to talk about it now," said Weill cautiously.

But Lewis needed a commitment of some kind. "I have to have an understanding that you won't take so much as a phone call from anyone else on this until we go through the possibility exhaustively ourselves," he said. He knew that if the Prudential bid set other companies looking for Wall Street partners, Weill's firm would be one of the most attractive.

"I won't accept a phone call from any other party," Weill said.

It was a crucial moment for Lewis. "The universe closed," he said. "There were three people in the room" — Weill, Robinson, and himself.

10

Sandy Lewis' black Mercedes splashed up to a nonde-script building on Beaver Street where S. B. Lewis & Company's offices were located. It was six-thirty on the morning of April 14, and what little life there was on the streets was being pelted by torrents of rain. Just beyond the car, a red and green neon sign in front of the Killarney Rose bar, a dank Irish pub, glimmered through the downpour.

Lewis stepped out of the car for a brief moment and then fell back into the rear seat. "Goddamn it!" he shouted. Willie Simmons, Lewis' driver and a man who usually seemed as serene as his boss seemed frenetic, waited for further instructions.

In addition to the impossible weather there was a variety of circumstances that were threatening to derail the merger he'd been working to bring about since the previous August. "Take me to Jim Robinson's office," Lewis said after a few seconds. The Mercedes crawled through the thick rain to the American Express building, just a few blocks away. Usually, Robinson began his work day about seven o'clock, but this morning he was in slightly earlier and was conferring with Alva Way when Lewis telephoned from the ground floor. To Lewis, the fact that the two men were already at work meant that they must have been discussing the proposed acquisition of Shearson and were trying to work out the problems that had cropped up during recent weeks.

It was twenty-five days since Prudential Life Insurance had announced its plans to take over Bache. That deal had changed the competitive balance in the financial business and succeeded in making Robinson and Weill actively interested in pursuing the amalgamation of their companies, but it had not eliminated the resistance each had earlier felt toward the merger. Robinson, naturally cautious and conservative, worried about getting his company into a risky and cyclical business. He continued to fret about possible retaliation by the banks that distributed his company's traveler's checks. And Robinson had reason to worry about Weill's ambition. The Wall Street entrepreneur was used to being king of the mountain and had, in one way or another, eliminated any rivals for that position. Weill, on his part, was uneasy about taking on both a new boss and the bureaucratic ways of a bigger and stodgier corporation.

Lewis, however, by this time seemed obsessed with making Shearson merge into American Express. "The idea should be like the sun," he once said. "It's a blinding light, it's so true." These almost religious terms accurately conveyed the significance of the merger to Lewis. It would establish S. B. Lewis & Company in the business of making mergers happen, thus setting it apart from the gaggle of arbitrage houses, which simply bet money on the takeovers others had engineered. Sandy Lewis would be seen, at last, as an influential figure in his father's world. Indeed, he recognized that the American Express merger would bring about a new era in American finance, ending the half-century of Wall Street history in which Cy Lewis and his contemporaries dominated the scene.

The negotiations had had an unusual character from the start. They were a continuous drama being written and directed by Lewis from his own experiences and strengths. His father's instinctive grasp of securities trading and Don Regan's vision of the new financial supermarkets helped, but it was Bruno Bettelheim who was the offstage muse throughout. For Lewis was working more with two men, Robinson and Weill, than with two corporations. Moreover, Lewis would have to move each to make him see the world differently. Here, it was Bettelheim's influence that armed Sandy Lewis with the skills that would make the merger happen.

Lewis' approach to deal-making was in many ways the opposite of that taken by other Wall Street financiers. Others focused on the business aspects of a merger — and assumed that the people would find a way to get along with each other. Others strenuously emphasized the advantages of a transaction, not the drawbacks. Lewis, shunning conventional salesmanship, assumed a psychoanalytic attitude. He was determined that Robinson and Weill know the worst about each other. Weill's insecurities, together with his hunger for power and prestige were almost legendary. He had dispensed with all the original partners with whom he'd launched his firm. He would have great difficulty within a large corporation where others called the shots. Robinson's ability to lead a company as large and varied as American Express was still considered unproven. His own acquisition efforts had mostly failed. Lewis wanted Weill and Robinson to form a bond, but he knew it would not hold unless their weak points were recognized.

Shortly after returning from their March tour of Shearson's Far East offices, the Weills had invited Jim and Bettye Robinson for Sunday brunch at their Greenwich home. Nestled in the gentle Connecticut hills amid an apple orchard, with a greenhouse and fastidiously trimmed box bushes, the place was a conspicuous reminder of how far Weill had come from his Brooklyn origins. Like the fireplace on the 106th floor of the World Trade Center, the trappings told him that, whatever his self-doubts, he had arrived financially. And, accordingly, Weill seemed to operate well in such settings. It was from this estate, after all, that he had two years earlier negotiated the takeover of Loeb Rhoades Hornblower, which was the consummation of a four-year strategy to "buy prestige" through the acquisition of well-known, though financially weak, Wall Street companies.

Now it was different. Robinson was in the driver's seat. And Weill, who had curtailed or interrupted the Wall Street careers of dozens of others, was looking to this man, and to his board, to set his own future at American Express. This made Weill uneasy, and his anxiety became evident even at this first, ostensibly social occasion.

Weill was a genial host, and Joan was a warm and bright partner. The Robinsons, too, could carry things off with an ease and grace that reflected both their Southern roots and the years they had spent attending "social" events that actually served some type of corporate purpose. Robinson could be friendly without revealing anything whatever of himself.

But the conviviality began to wear thin shortly after the meal was finished. The wives left their husbands to focus on things that had had little place among the pleasantries of table conversation. Alone with the man who might become his boss — his first in a decade — Weill quickly dropped the persona of the self-assured corporate host. The street fighter in him re-emerged. What exactly would his role be at American Express? What sort of power base would he have? Weill made it clear that he wasn't interested in a merger that would simply tuck Shearson inside American Express. He meant to enhance his own status as an executive; he wanted to do more than chair an American Express subsidiary. Robinson, however, wasn't ready to commit himself. He said vaguely that Weill's role at American Express would depend on many things. Then he added that Weill would have to "prove himself" to the American Express board. Weill recoiled. He had built the most profitable publicly held securities firm in the country, and somebody wanted him to prove himself?

Nothing was resolved that day. Robinson, whom one friend had described as "spending half his life on an airplane," had a flight to catch that afternoon. The brunch ended, and Weill was left to brood about things.

Robinson had his own worries. As the merger talks progressed, he sought an audience with Marshall Cogan, the driving force in Weill's firm in the late 1960s and the man Weill had supplanted in 1973 as chief executive. Cogan loathed Weill. He felt that over the years his former partner had taken full credit for the growth of a firm that he, Cogan, had had a crucial role in building. But Cogan fended off Robinson's calls until the merger was consummated, at which point he did meet Robinson for lunch to discuss Weill. Cogan had hesitated to meet him before then because he wanted the merger to happen. Among other things, it would vastly increase the value of thousands of Shearson shares he'd hung on to since leaving.

In early April, Sandy Lewis telephoned Weill during a weekend and sensed that the Shearson chairman was beginning to lose his taste for the merger. The idea of working for Robinson at American Express apparently was unsettling;

the position seemed alien to him, now that he had achieved his present status. Lewis immediately arranged to have a private plane fly him from Morristown, near his New Jersey home, to Greenwich.

When he arrived, Weill was swilling martinis. He wasn't sure that the merger would be right for him, he said. After all, he was already one of the most powerful executives in the financial business. Shearson didn't have to merge. Weill didn't have to work for another man and another company. Of course, Weill was torn: if he made it at American Express, he would have the prestige he always lacked at Shearson.

Lewis urged Weill to think about what he and Robinson could do for one another. "Jim will start to live again," he said, stressing that the entrepreneurial types from Shearson would inject needed vitality into the somewhat somnolent American Express. Lewis argued that it would be a chance for Weill to back off a bit from the intense, often cutthroat world of Wall Street, to let go of the business that had gripped him since the late 1950s.

In some ways, the Shearson chief's career resembled that of Cy Lewis. Some of the same hectic spirit of the 1920s, when Cy Lewis had arrived on Wall Street, prevailed in the 1960s, when Weill got his start. As each attained success, he seemed always to be reaching for a telephone to work on the next deal. For both, financial success seemed addictive.

Weill, however, needed American Express to promise something that would make it worth his while to step away from the controlling position, and nearly $30 million worth of American Express common stock wasn't enough. Robinson would also have to appeal to Weill's desire for prestige by giving him a publicly recognized role at the company.

Lewis was determined that Robinson should see it this way, too. On his way to the American Express offices on the morning of April 14, Lewis thought about what Weill needed from Robinson in order to bring himself to sell Shearson. When he arrived in Robinson's office, still wet and cold from the rain, he spoke eloquently about how the drive and raw ambitions of the Brooklyn entrepreneurs at Shearson would benefit both American Express and its chairman. During the conversation in Robinson's office, it was agreed that Weill would remain chairman of Shearson and, with an additional title, would assume responsibility for American Express's investment and financial activities. Although this would make the merger prospect more inviting to Weill, it wouldn't solve all the problems. The matter of his exact title, for example, was a ticklish issue.

The executive suite at American Express was already rather crowded. Alva Way, formerly the chief financial officer at General Electric, had just been named president of American Express. Then there was Louis Gerstner, a successful vice president in charge of the card division and the travel services, who was viewed as the fastest-rising young executive in the company. There was also Myron DuBain, who ran Fireman's Fund, the company's insurance subsidiary and the largest single contributor to American Express's revenue. From a distance it looked as if Weill would be hurling himself back into the melee he had known at Cogan, Berlind, Weill & Levitt. And Weill wasn't sure he wanted this rivalry again.

Lewis remained convinced that the move would be good for Weill. It would give him a chance to think creatively about all financial services, not just brokerage, and it would provide him a respite from the pressures of the securities business.

Lewis told Robinson that he felt it was important to talk as soon as possible with Weill, who was on business in Los Angeles. Robinson agreed to have the American Express plane poised on the West Coast to bring Lewis and Weill back to New York. Lewis then caught a noon flight out of Kennedy Airport. Once in Los Angeles, he drove to the Century Plaza, where Weill was making a speech. Weill was a good speaker in the same way that he was a good manager. He wasn't entirely confident in either role, but instead of making people uncomfortable, his uncertainty created empathy. With his kid-from-Brooklyn-makes-good manner and his prodigious ability, he evoked affection and admiration.

After the meeting, Weill spotted Lewis, who was beginning to seem ubiquitous. He suggested that they have a drink and dinner, but Lewis, who had a migraine headache, went directly to bed. He preferred to start their discussion the following morning, when they would be together on the American Express jet.

Weill recognized that the combination of Shearson and American Express would make sense strategically: Shearson could piggyback the marketing techniques of the parent company; American Express cards could be used to facilitate investment transactions; American Express could help Shearson broaden its customer base. The problems centered on people. Weill wondered about the response of Peter Cohen, his right-hand man, George Sheinberg, his top financial officer, and Hardwick Simmons, his marketing chief. There were a dozen other key Shearson executives whose full endorsement of the merger would be necessary if it was to succeed. If Weill shifted his responsibilities to management tasks at American Express, he would need the assurance that Shearson was being well tended.

Weill had reason to worry about whether his top management would support the merger. The Shearson executives generally doubted whether the practices and attitudes at American Express would be compatible with theirs. Bonuses would shrink, they feared; tedious memos would pile up. The Shearson camp was also skeptical of Robinson. "Too polished," one Shearson man said following a get-acquainted meeting with Robinson that Lewis had arranged.

The people who operated in the top tier at Shearson already

had many advantages: considerable flexibility and generous compensation, often involving large options to buy the surging Shearson stock. And they had the satisfaction of being the survivors of merger after merger. The American Express plan raised doubts about whether they could continue to operate as independently as they had. Their Shearson stock had soared steadily since 1974; could they count on shares in American Express to do the same?

It became awkward for Weill to act as an advocate for the merger. The nearly $30 million of American Express stock he would acquire was considerably more than any of the top Shearson executives would receive.

To help make sure that Shearson wouldn't be smothered by American Express, Lewis, Weill, and Robinson agreed informally in mid April that Peter Cohen would be given a board position at the parent company, along with Weill. This helped win over Cohen, who had been skeptical about the deal. However, the American Express board, in a secret meeting, nixed this plan, opting to take on Weill only.

The flipflop enraged Cohen, who had worked side by side with Weill since the latter became chief executive of the company. Also, the switch made it appear that Robinson hadn't been negotiating in good faith when he promised Cohen the position. The move also smacked of snobbery, as though the American Express directors didn't want too many of the Brooklyn-bred crowd on the board. Yet Cohen, the thirty-four-year-old whiz kid, was crucial to the success of the transaction. It was Cohen who would keep Shearson on course while Weill was involved in running the financial empire at American Express. Cohen had turned aside offers from others, including the Belzbergs, who wanted him to run Bache if they succeeded in buying it. And he wouldn't lack for other opportunities should the American Express situation prove not to be to his liking.

As the Shearson people groused about Robinson, they seemed to be operating from reverse snobbism. Among members of the American Express board, there were some growls of disdain. Howard Clark, Sr., the retired chairman, voiced opposition, and it became necessary for Robinson to dispatch Howard Clark, Jr., one of the financial wizards of the company, to fly the American Express jet to Hobe Sound, Florida, to convince his father, and several other board members who were living there in retirement, of the value of the plan. Sandy Weill wasn't a figure likely to engender feelings of friendship in an enclave like Hobe Sound.

On Thursday, April 16, Wall Street began to hear an utterly flabbergasting rumor — Sandy Weill was talking to American Express about selling Shearson. The rumor seemed far-fetched to many: Shearson wasn't considered a takeover target, as Bache had been. Moreover, the atmosphere at Shearson seemed the polar opposite of the corporate environment at American Express. However, stockbrokers began to load up on Shearson's shares on the chance that American Express might indeed buy the profitable securities house at a hefty premium. Shearson's stock closed on Thursday at $42.75, up $4.00 from the previous day's close.

That night, Lewis, Weill, and some of the Shearson executives retired to Weill's apartment, where Joan Weill was keeping reporters at bay on the phone. Weill said, when he got there, "We don't comment on rumors." All he would confirm was that Shearson and American Express were talking about setting up a cash management service that would give access to a Shearson investment account to a customer holding an American Express gold card. But, he pointed out, American Express was making the same arrangement with E. F. Hutton and Bache. Something else appeared to be happening with Shearson, the reporters insisted. Was there talk of doing more than just setting up the cash management service? Would there be a full merger? Weill wasn't saying. The following morning, however, the *Wall Street Journal* and the *New York Times* said there might be.

That day, Good Friday, was quiet; the exchanges were closed for the holiday, and the financial community was essentially shut down. Vacant Wall Street was enveloped in a thick mist, with Trinity Church rising out of the fog.

At about nine-thirty A.M., Sandy Lewis' Mercedes pulled up in front of the New York Stock Exchange on Broad Street. Sandy was at the wheel, Willie Simmons was beside him in the front seat, and Oliver and John Benjamin, two of his sons, were in the back. Lewis had had only a few hours sleep and was worried about being late to the Good Friday meetings, which was why he had insisted that he drive, rather than Willie. Just inside Manhattan after emerging from the Holland Tunnel, he had hurtled over a deep pothole and smashed the oil pan of the car. By the time he pulled into Wall Street, the car was leaking oil. Lewis directed his driver to call his garage in Englewood and have them send a flatbed truck to rescue the ailing Mercedes. Then, with Oliver and John Benjamin in tow, he rushed to meet Dwight (Buzzy) Faulkner, who had come to Shearson via Faulkner, Dawkins & Sullivan in 1977 and knew Weill very well.

Robinson had asked Lewis to speak with Faulkner alone later that morning to discuss Weill. What might make Weill back out and what would assure his support? Lewis was also going to talk with Weill and Cohen. Much of the Good Friday discussions involved corporate geography. Was Weill going to be part of Robinson's chairman's office? Would others from Shearson move, too? Who exactly answered to whom, and on what issues? Different plans were explored, but none took on a definite shape. The issues discussed were enormously important to Weill and Robinson, and consumed considerably more negotiating time than the financial terms of the $1 billion merger. After all, Weill had initially wanted the presidency of American Express. That seemed a long way off.

On the same day, Prudential's tender offer for Bache officially closed, and the giant insurer held more than enough shares to assume control. (The Belzbergs hadn't tendered their holdings but would sell them, at a profit of about $40 million, in June, when Prudential completed the takeover with the involuntary purchase of all remaining shares.)

On Saturday, April 18, Weill's top aides drove out to Greenwich to hash through the merger some more. During the early part of the meeting, most of what was said was negative. "A lot of people didn't want to do it," Weill remembered later. "One said, 'Why do this? In five years we'll be bigger.'" Shearson's growth rate, if it continued into the 1980s, suggested that this appraisal wasn't far off the mark. But for Weill, one thing had become clear: there were going to be mergers of other companies. Knowing that companies, particularly Wall Street companies, moved in lock step, Weill couldn't help believing that there would be other Wall Street acquisitions. "Pru bought Bache," Weill said. "In this country, big companies play follow-the-leader. More mergers are going to happen." So Weill posed the question "How are we going to feel if Hutton does it with Express?" That query helped dissolve the residue of opposition. Nobody at Shearson wanted to risk being left behind in the march toward conglomeration in finance.

On Easter Sunday, Weill, Lewis, Robinson, and several attorneys met at the offices of Skadden Arps, American Express's lawyers on merger negotiations. It was agreed that American Express would extend 1.3 shares of its stock for each share of Shearson common stock. This translated into a price of about $50 a share for the Shearson stock, which had been trading in the thirties. Weill, with 456,824 shares of Shearson, would keep the greatest personal profit from the deal.

For 217 Shearson employees who had options to buy, in aggregate, 300,000 shares at $34.25 apiece, the merger represented an immediate windfall of about $10 million. The single greatest beneficiary of this package was Peter Cohen, who held options to buy twenty thousand shares; his profit would be more than $700,000.

The generosity to Cohen was an acknowledgment of the crucial role he had played over the years. But before the options agreement was made final, Cohen had been involved in some transactions that would have shut him out of at least part of the profits that other top executives of the securities house were poised to rake in. He had sold a substantial chunk of his Shearson stock the previous September, partly to finance construction of a lavish summer home in East Hampton. The securities laws prohibit a top executive from moving in and out of his own company's stock, since by virtue of his inside knowledge of corporate developments, he would be in a position to take advantage of short-term fluctuations in the stock price. Thus, having sold the shares, Cohen couldn't buy them back until March 24, six months from the date of sale. On that date, Cohen happened to be in Israel with his wife. He telephoned the Shearson offices in New York and left instructions for 10,002 shares to be bought for his account. Two days later, the merger talks began, and Cohen was snagged by another securities law, one that required insiders like him to pour back profit earned on purchases made within six months of a corporate merger. The trading required complex disclosures, and without the options granted him in April, Cohen would have been left with skimpier winnings on the American Express merger than Weill and other Shearson executives.

On Monday, April 20, following the Easter weekend talks, Shearson asked the New York Stock Exchange to halt trading in its stock, pending an announcement. As speculation grew about the details of the American Express deal, Shearson brokers and employees throughout the company's sprawling system were bewildered. Many had assumed that Weill's firm couldn't be bought out by anyone. At American Express, board members gathered in the afternoon to make their decision. There were still worries about how banks would respond, and there were jitters about entering the fast-moving securities business. There were also the previous concerns, based perhaps on mere snobbery, about Weill and the entrepreneurs at Shearson. Just who were they?

At six o'clock that evening, Robinson called Weill to say the board had approved the merger. Both Cohen and Weill would have board seats. Weill, however, would not serve as chief operating officer but would remain chairman of Shearson and be part of a "chairman's office" at the parent company, with responsibility for financial activities. He would have to surrender a position of unquestioned primacy for one that was riddled with uncertainties.

Once again, Weill felt unsure that he could live with the gamble. It might lead to his having considerably more power than he did on Wall Street, but there was no guarantee. Believing it by no means too late to change his mind, he telephoned Joan to come down to his offices to talk it over. Robinson, sensing that Weill was wavering, hurried over also. He and Joan arrived at the World Trade Center at the same time and rode together to the 106th floor. Lewis, the go-between, was already there; he moved at maximum velocity from room to room, talking first with Robinson, then Weill and Joan, then Robinson again, attempting to explain each man to the other. He was not sure that he was succeeding. Although all of Wall Street assumed there would soon be an announcement of the merger terms, the entire deal seemed to teeter.

The standoff didn't involve anything new. Weill wanted

to be named president of American Express or a clear number two to Robinson. Lacking such a position, he would have to trust Robinson. That was difficult for Weill. For twenty years, he had succeeded by looking over his shoulder, watching for something to go wrong or for someone to undercut him. Lewis tried to calm Weill's misgivings. A particular job title at American Express was irrelevant, he felt. Weill, with his entrepreneurial instincts, could remake American Express, and he would be rewarded for that in time. Lewis knew that it was Weill's habit to consult with, and even defer to, his wife on the nonfinancial aspects of his business life, and so he sought to work through Joan. He took her aside and told her, "If you can't trust Robinson, you can't trust anybody on this earth." To some, the American Express chief may have seemed so polished as to be unreadable, but Lewis, perhaps remembering the visit Robinson had paid him years earlier, after Lewis was fired by White Weld, trusted Robinson's decency and fairness.

But Weill simply wasn't ready to sell. He was a man who had given little energy to fostering interests outside his work. Indeed, Weill's identity was tightly enmeshed with Shearson's. Now, as Lewis and the lawyers and executives from the two companies paced anxiously around Shearson's headquarters, Weill secluded himself with Joan and Robinson in the sitting room adjacent to his office. There was no more to say about the price of the transaction, the structure of the combined companies, or the emerging vision of a modern financial services business. It was a matter of whether the two men could create a partnership. The final sizing-up had begun.

It was a faceoff. Weill wanted to know what Robinson really thought about the vast amount of American Express stock Weill would inherit as a result of the merger, especially since Weill's holdings would be many times greater than

Robinson's. Weill looked hard at Robinson. "What's your net worth?" he demanded. Robinson, who wasn't used to this sort of blunt questioning, responded that though he was a wealthy man, he didn't have the tens of millions Weill would have after the merger. Would this breed jealousy? Weill wondered. On Wall Street, people's success is measured by their net worth, and disparities often create bitter conflicts. Would Robinson try to keep a lid on Weill's advancement at American Express? Robinson insisted that Weill would rise quickly in the hierarchy. The board just needed a little time to get used to him. Weill wasn't sure. He looked at his wife. "Do you believe him?" he asked.

The differences between the two chairmen had never been more pronounced. Weill was emotional and tough-talking; Robinson was cool and diplomatic. It happened that Joan Weill did believe his assurances. Bolstered by her confidence in the merger, Weill agreed to go ahead with the merger as it had been worked out over the weekend. A few final details were completed by the teams from both companies. Lawyers double-checked the language of the agreement. Press advisers for the two firms readied announcements for the following morning. The two sides shook hands, and at about eleven o'clock the Shearson kitchen staff began preparing a dinner of steaks and champagne. Robinson, who was busy conferring with his own executives and those of Shearson, missed the meal entirely. Someone later had to slap together a sandwich for the chairman.

At nine o'clock on Tuesday, April 21, Weill, though flooded with morning-after doubts, addressed Shearson's thirty-eight hundred brokers over the company's nationwide speaker phone. Haltingly, in a low, somewhat pinched voice, he began to explain the rationale behind the merger: Shearson was linking itself to proven prestige and marketing power; it would be a stronger entity. Suddenly, the explanation ceased, and Weill began sobbing.

At nine-fifteen, the announcement went out over the news wires.

On June 29, 1984, the shareholders of both American Express and Shearson convened to vote on the merger plan. Weill, visibly nervous, stepped to a podium in a large room in the World Trade Center. He flashed a grin and joked, "It's amazing what one has to do to get a crowd." Laughter spread through the audience. Then he said, "Welcome to the wedding." More laughter, applause. Shearson stockholders had grown richer faster than they had ever thought likely; everybody naturally wanted to cheer Sandy Weill, the self-made Wall Street millionaire who never forgot his beginnings. A decade earlier, the Shearson stock had traded as low as sixty-three cents a share. Weill said, "This is no last hurrah. We're asking for your endorsement for what Jim Robinson called a new era on Wall Street." Arthur Levitt and Marshall Cogan, both of whom had remained large shareholders in Shearson, expected that Weill would publicly recognize the role each had played in building up Shearson during the 1960s and early 1970s, but he didn't. He was enjoying the spotlight.

When Weill opened the meeting to questions from the floor, a man in the audience asked if the merged company was to be renamed Shearson American Express. Weill smiled. "Not yet," he said. To some of the American Express board members, this seemed bad form. Weill came off as too eager to expand his power base in American Express. The American Express shareholders, meanwhile, approved the merger plan at a separate, more sedate meeting.

That afternoon, Weill and Robinson, each sporting an American Express necktie, granted an audience to select members of the financial press. Robinson was pink-cheeked, scrubbed, and composed; Weill looked somewhat ravaged and worn. At about three-thirty, Weill rose and said that he was going to the floor of the New York Stock Exchange to watch the Shearson stock trade for the last time. Robinson looked quizzical. He seemed not to understand such a trip, which was sentimental, even purposeless. But, then, the marriage — if it could be called one — was a union of opposites.

On April 23, two nights after the deal was agreed to in the Shearson headquarters, the Robinsons and Weills took Sandy and Barbara Lewis to dinner at "21." There, Lewis gave Robinson and Weill each a copy of Bettelheim's *Love Is Not Enough*. On the flyleaf, Lewis had written, "Without this fellow, our deal would never have been."

11

What followed was a rash of mergers, caused by a combination of factors. Securities firms experienced a strong urge to expand. There were huge costs associated with building an efficient data-processing system capable of handling the enormous trading volume; some days saw a hundred million shares change hands on the Big Board alone. Overhead costs — postage, leases, and communications expenses — all rose relentlessly. The logical solution for nationwide brokerage operations was to expand even further. It was like the "salami slicer" theory popular at Shearson during the 1970s: push more and more transactions through the system and spread the fixed costs. Only, in 1981 firms were moving beyond securities transactions to offer tax shelters, savings vehicles, and annuities, and these required greater capital resources.

Also, the herd mentality sometimes took hold in the financial business. Wall Street is said to be populated not only by bulls and bears, but also by sheep and pigs. Some viewed their survival to be a matter of safety in numbers.

And some responded to a more basic instinct — greed. Shearson and Bache had both fetched prices that were more than twice their book value. Since the publicly owned securities firms had been partnerships and private corporations a decade earlier, the biggest shareholders were usually the top managers. Merging into some larger and more richly capitalized corporation was a way for them to cash in.

In the months following the announcement of joining American Express and Shearson, there was intense soul-searching at Salomon Brothers, where both Sandy and Cy Lewis had gotten their first jobs on Wall Street. It was the industry's largest private partnership, with sixty-two general partners and nearly $300 million in capital. But compared to a Goliath like American Express, whose assets were greater than $20 billion, it seemed miniature.

John Gutfreund had succeeded Billy Salomon in 1978 and assumed the helm of the powerful securities house. He was a rare Wall Street liberal and had actively supported George McGovern's and Jimmy Carter's presidential campaigns. Gutfreund was aloof in demeanor and resolutely tight-lipped when it came to Salomon's business. He quickly ended a Salomon practice of revealing some sketchy data on yearly earnings. As a result, Salomon's profits or losses became the subject of endless speculation and gossip around Wall Street. But Gutfreund had begun to concede in 1981 that there might be reasons to reconsider Salomon's functioning as a private partnership. "We're probably an anachronism in this day and age," he said. Other firms about the same size — E. F. Hutton, Shearson, Paine Webber — had all gone public during the early 1970s. Partnerships on the scale of Salomon could be unwieldy. Salomon — with some twenty-five hundred employees — was too large to function as a family enterprise and had begun to take on the characterisics of a medium-size American corporation.

Those firms such as Salomon which remained private after the Wall Street turmoil of the early 1970s had been forced to take steps to protect their capital. During the 1970s, Billy Salomon had created a network of house regulations that had the effect of keeping the partners' money inside the firm. If a partner left, his money stayed behind, to be doled out over a period of several years. And most of the riches of the vastly wealthy Salomon partners were locked up in a Salomon account. In fact, many saw their take-home income drop immediately after they became partners. A non-partner might be paid as much as $200,000, but a new partner would draw a salary of $80,000, plus a small level of interest on his Salomon account.

Gutfreund quickly shelved Billy Salomon's belief that traders should accommodate the big institutional clients even when particular transactions disadvantaged Salomon. "Bad trades beget good trades" had for years been Salomon's motto. Gutfreund viewed things differently. "The markets have not been benign," he said. "The nature of the equity markets is that you are rarely buying what you want to buy or selling what you want to sell. You're on the other side of what informed financial institutions have decided to trade." Salomon built its corporate finance business around its trading room. In pitching itself to corporations, the firm would roll out figures showing its staggering trading positions. Of the big companies that had switched from traditional underwriting managers during the 1970s, Salomon had lured about half, including IBM, International Paper, Chase Manhattan, and General Tire and Rubber.

Perhaps the truest measure of Salomon's prowess as an investment banker was that the newcomers were making themselves felt as a distinct threat, even to the long-standing doyen, Morgan Stanley. Salomon Brothers was used to the cutthroat competition of Wall Street and actually enjoyed it as a rule. What seemed unusual, not only to Salomon but to other firms, was the unprecedented volatility exhibited in virtually all the financial markets in late 1980 and early 1981. Gutfreund, like others close to the bond markets, was fond of saying that the credit machinery had entered an entirely new era. "We find ourselves torn asunder from a past it is useless to yearn for," Gutfreund said in the May 1980 issue of *Euromoney* magazine.

Inflation, of course, was a major cause of the metamorphosis of the credit markets. Borrowers — governments or corporations — were forced to the marketplace to raise cash simply to keep up with inflation. The credit market in the United States stood at $1.4 trillion in 1969, and by 1979 it was $3.8 trillion. Gutfreund predicted that by the end of the 1980s the total credit market debt would be $10.2 trillion. A debtor society, of course, meant heavy volume for Wall Street's premier bond house.

But the credit markets weren't simply getting larger. They were becoming more treacherous. Bonds, once a sleepy investment, had been on a roller coaster since October 1979, when the Federal Reserve Board had moved to let interest rates rise or fall where they would and to concentrate on controlling the money supply. During 1980, the consequences of the new Fed approach were clear. Short-term rates, which had historically moved infrequently and in small increments, followed a spastic course: they raced from 14 percent in February 1980 to 19 percent in April, only to cascade back down, all the way to 9 percent in July and August, and then shoot back up again to about 20 percent at year's end. Long-term bonds, bearing lower rates by current standards, plummeted in value, and short-term investments, particularly the consumer-oriented money market funds, zoomed up in popularity.

Beyond this, there was what Gutfreund referred to as "total relativity." The markets moved more closely in sync with one another. In fact, all the components of the credit markets — corporate, municipal, and federal government debt — had a more visible impact on one another. Moreover, with the dollar no longer functioning as the world's currency standard, shifts in a foreign government's budget could send ripple effects through the credit systems of other countries by creating worldwide changes in currency relationships.

People heard about market changes and reacted to them faster because information systems were more sophisticated than could have been imagined ten years earlier. Traders could summon up on desktop terminals data about financial events that took place minutes before on opposite sides of the globe. The market's ability to absorb and respond to relevant financial information had accelerated, and not only was change occurring at a faster clip, but market participants were learning of events and reacting to them faster than ever. "High volatility demands that we emphasize quality, liquidity, and rapid turnover," Gutfreund said, glancing toward the huge trading room. "If the average shelf life of one of our positions is twenty-eight minutes, I'd be pleased."

Salomon's chief economist, Henry Kaufman, had become arguably the most influential financial forecaster in the world. He was a small, owlish man, who spoke in a calm, resonant voice. In his measured fashion, he issued generally catastrophic prognoses of financial markets. In London, the traders dubbed him "Dr. Doom" for the sometimes punishing effect his words had on the Eurobond markets. Kaufman, formerly an economist with the Federal Reserve Bank of New York, spoke with an authority based on a string of accurate predictions in the credit markets. In November 1977, for example, Kaufman predicted that rates on new issues of triple-A-rated utilities would rise from 8.3 percent to 8.8 percent or 9 percent in 1978. In May 1978, rates on those issues climbed to 8.8 percent, then rose higher. In August 1978, Kaufman predicted that interest rates would rise in coming weeks. The following month, rates began a relentless push upward. In December 1979, Kaufman made the stunning prediction that interest rates would soar to a postwar record during the first half of 1980. In April of that year, the prime rate hit a postwar peak of 20 percent, short- and long-term bond rates having tipped postwar records the previous month.

By 1981, Kaufman was more than a forecaster. Because traders throughout the world regarded his pronouncements as revealed truths, they scurried to buy or sell in anticipation of what Mr. Kaufman would say. His words sometimes thus became self-fulfilling prophecies.

By late 1980, Dr. Doom was beginning to live up to his nickname. As interest rates charged upward, bonds carrying lower rates took a drubbing. In an interview on ABC's "Issues and Answers" in December 1980, Kaufman said about interest rates: "There are no benchmarks anymore by which we can judge just how high interest rates can go. Quantification is impossible . . . I'd have to say the chances are, with a prime rate of 20 1/2 percent, it could go to 22, 23, 24 percent before we top out." Given Salomon's multibillion-dollar presence in the bond markets, nerves in and around the Room were becoming frayed.

In contrast to bonds, stocks had enjoyed a robust surge in price through most of 1980, partly because institutions were fleeing the suddenly perilous debt markets. Oil stocks, following the cutoff of petroleum from Iran in 1979, had soared; and relatively trendy issues, such as genetic-engineering companies, had also experienced rapid run-ups. But by the end of the year, stocks too were behaving strangely. The stock market was unnerved by the highly unusual "supply-side" economic program being advanced by Ronald Reagan. This was proposed as a cure for the economic ills afflicting the country, but many financial experts found the program to be confusing and contradictory.

The Reagan administration's plan involved these elements: a massive, across-the-board tax cut of as much as 30 percent; a huge increase in military expenditures together with a cutback in certain social programs; and, behind everything, the tight monetary policy of the Federal Reserve Board chief, Paul Volcker. The program put into effect tax cuts that appeared to deplete the federal coffers at a time when heavy defense spending was drawing on them at rates unequaled in any peacetime period in U.S. history. The supply-side assumption, however, was that the tax cuts would stimulate the economy, expanding jobs and output, so that more tax dollars actually would flow to the government. The program relied on the acceptance of this assumption by the business and financial community. But Wall Street wanted proof. In early 1981, the chief concern was that the program would create huge federal deficits and would oblige the U.S. Treasury to borrow massively in the credit markets, pushing up interest rates and squeezing out private-sector borrowers.

The markets continued to worsen in early 1981. Wall Street believed that it was imprudent of the government to slash taxes before bringing the federal budget more nearly into balance. There had been the hope that Donald Regan, the former Merrill Lynch chairman who was then Secretary of the Treasury, would convince others in the administration of this view, but he had found himself surrounded by supply-side dogmatists and had himself become a convert, if only to ensure his political future.

In this troubled atmosphere, Salomon and other big-dollar

players moved gingerly. The explosion of financial futures — contracts tied to Treasury bills or other credit instruments — gave traders the means to hedge their positions against future lurches in interest rates. The proliferation of new financial instruments provided one way for Salomon to spread its risks and to protect itself against sudden shifts in particular securities. But some years earlier the firm had turned to ventures outside the securities markets to gain additional, sometimes more dependable, sources of income. These ventures, all carried out in utmost secrecy, sometimes involved real estate but more often involved oil. Salomon's executive committee, which included Gutfreund, Kaufman, and six or seven others, would sniff out prospective side investments. The committee would then solicit participation from some, but not all, the other partners, and would manage the side investment with complete autonomy, distributing gains to the participants. Much of the profit these partners received, of course, would have to remain in the firm, serving to beef up its capital, which by 1981 stood at about $360 million.

In May 1981, Salomon served as adviser to Engelhard Minerals and Chemicals, a big industrial group of which the Anglo-American Corporation of South Africa owned 27 percent, in its move to spin off Phibro, the largest commodities trading operation in the world. During the negotiations, Phibro's chairman, David Tendler, and president, Hal Beretz, suggested to a Salomon partner, Richard Rosenthal, that the two companies consider merging. Rosenthal, a member of Salomon's executive committee, got Gutfreund's nod to explore the prospect further and to bring in Ira Harris, Salomon's merger virtuoso. By this time, both the American Express and the Prudential deals had taken place, and Harris felt that the securities business in general was experiencing an upheaval.

The two concerns had some similarities: both took huge

risks in the marketplace, Salomon trading various securities, and Phibro trading about 150 raw materials and commodities. Salomon's partners had veered from securities trading into energy on special projects; Phibro was a global player in the oil markets (crude and refined petroleum products accounted for more than half of the $23.6 billion it generated in revenue in 1980). For its part, Phibro was interested in trading financial instruments. Phibro and Salomon each had a German-Jewish family heritage, and each was known for attracting talented traders through big payouts.

Secret meetings between Phibro and Salomon were held at the Regency and the Waldorf. And by late July, Salomon's executive committee, without the knowledge of other partners at the firm, was convening daily to discuss the merger.

On July 31, Salomon's sixty-two partners were summoned to a weekend meeting at the Tarrytown Convention Center in Westchester County. The meeting itself, although billed as a normal quarterly partners' meeting to review the business, seemed odd: it was to last the entire weekend, and it was occurring later than usual for a quarterly review. At six-thirty on Friday, July 31, the Salomon partners settled into seats in an auditorium in the North Tennis House at the Tarrytown Center. Gutfreund quickly dispelled recent rumors of his losses by announcing that for the first ten months of its fiscal year, Salomon had racked up operating profits that broke previous records. He then informed the room that Salomon's executive committee had voted unanimously to dissolve the seventy-one-year-old partnership by folding Salomon Brothers into the publicly owned Phibro. The partners would have the remainder of the weekend to ratify the executive committee's decision. Under the terms of the merger, Salomon's general partners and its twenty-nine limited partners, who weren't involved in active responsibilities, would be able to pull their money out. Phibro would replace the partners' capital by shoving in $300 million of its own. In addition, Phibro would give the general partners a premium in the form of $250 million in 9 percent bonds convertible into Phibro common stock over five years. Since the distribution of the convertible bonds was tied to each partner's level of ownership, the executive committee members would rake in the highest amounts — $75 million altogether, or about $11 million apiece. That, together with the cash the partners would be pulling out of the firm, meant a rather glorious take. Gutfreund would bring home cash and debentures that added up to about $32 million. On average, each Salomon partner would take $7.8 million.

By midmorning Sunday, all of the partners had signed employment contracts with Phibro. Golden handcuffs devised to keep Salomon's newly liquid partners from working elsewhere included five-year noncompete promises for the executive committee members and three-year lock-ins for other partners.

With the deal ratified, Salomon's chiefs faced the awkward task of telling Billy Salomon, the sixty-seven-year-old former managing partner. From the time he had passed the mantle to Gutfreund in 1978, Salomon came to the firm each day but was no longer actively involved in management. When the Phibro talks first got under way, Gutfreund and the other Salomon executives had decided neither to seek Billy Salomon's advice nor inform him of the deal until it was a fait accompli. They knew he would oppose it and would try to swing other partners to do so, too. However, once the partnership had agreed to dissolve itself, Gutfreund, Kaufman, and Richard Schmeelk, the executive committee member in charge of corporate finance, flew to Southampton to tell Salomon.

By summer of 1981, the world was changing faster than anyone on Wall Street could have predicted. A month after the American Express takeover agreement for Shearson was made known, there was an unexpected buyout at Dillon Read. This gentlemanly investment bank, built up in the 1920s by the baronial Clarence Dillon, was controlled for decades by him and other members of his family, including his son, C. Douglas Dillon, the former U.S. Secretary of the Treasury. James Forrestal, the former Secretary of Defense, had also been a prominent partner at the firm. But in 1981, Dillon Read had an air of faded glory. Firms like Merrill Lynch, with its unequaled retail sales force, and Salomon, with its institutional traders, had become major forces in the underwriting business. The older investment banks, like Morgan Stanley and First Boston, had expanded hugely, adding to capital, beefing up trading operations, and creating high-powered merger groups. Dillon Read, housed in elegant but small headquarters just off Wall Street, had remained essentially the same. In 1981, it had only about $30 million in capital, a negligible trading operation, no research department at all, and no retail branches. Superior Oil, CPC International, and others had left Dillon Read's roster of corporate clients to do business with other houses. The firm's place in the financial world was uncertain; moreover, the Dillon family wanted to back out, since none of its members retained an active interest in the securities business, which was becoming too risky to leave unshepherded. Nicholas Brady, Dillon Read's chairman, met in late April with the Bechtel family, which controlled the Bechtel Group, the San Francisco–based construction and engineering firm. A deal was announced the following week that linked Dillon Read to Bechtel. Stephen D. Bechtel, Jr., the group's chairman, possessed a personal fortune estimated at $200 million, but it paled in comparison with the $750 million fortune his father was believed to have. The controlling investment in Dillon Read was made by Sequoia Ventures, an investment arm of the Bechtel Group. "There is a revolution going on in the Street," Brady said. "This alliance allows us to come up with our plans and act on them."

The Bechtel–Dillon Read deal was an unusual one, given the dissimilar business activities of the partners. Nor was it a particularly inspired fit. In early 1983, the alliance partly unraveled; the Bechtels chopped their ownership to an unspecified minority interest, and Dillon Read's key employees bought the majority interest in the company. In 1981, however, the union served to underscore the point that Wall Street's long-revered separate identity was gone.

With Bache, Shearson, Salomon, and Dillon Read all tucked into large concerns outside the traditional securities business, financial people were talking about who would go next. Rumors of takeover centered on Dean Witter Reynolds, the fifth largest Wall Street firm, with about $279 million in capital, and the product itself of seventeen mergers over the years.

During the summer of 1981, the company's stock repeatedly rose on reports that Dean Witter Reynolds was soon to be gobbled up. At various times, the firm had held exploratory merger talks with American Express, Travelers Insurance Companies, Marsh and MacLennan, and Transamerica Corporation, but none of the deals had gotten off the ground. Robert M. Gardiner, the firm's president, had spent a career merging with other companies to build a bigger and bigger capital base; he was troubled that summer not so much by the threat of a takeover as by the fact that he hadn't received a single telephone call from a prospective suitor.

On August 19, Gardiner's secretary told him that a Mr. Hills was on the telephone. Gardiner took the call with an unusually genial hello, having assumed that Mr. Hills was a Texas oil man he'd known for years. It wasn't. The Mr. Hills on the telephone was Roderick Hills, the former Securities and Exchange Commission chairman and a limited partner of Sandy Lewis in S. B. Lewis & Company. Hills had a proposition to discuss with Gardiner: Would Dean Witter be interested in being bought by Sears Roebuck? Hills, who had been close to Sears for years and was one of its senior outside attorneys, was now the strategist for its push into the financial business. Sears had concluded that its traditional merchandising business wasn't likely to grow as fast as it had in the past, and was determined to stand alongside Merrill Lynch and American Express as a financial company.

On September 1, the Sears chairman, Edward Telling, announced a money market trust to be sold to Sears customers. Telling declared, "Our goal is to become the largest financial services' entity." This was an odd statement for a retailer. Sears did own the Allstate insurance group, which included a savings institution that was then beset by the problems afflicting the entire thrift business, and Seraco, a small real estate unit. But Sears was still not a financial company, and the money trust Telling referred to couldn't transform it into one. There surely was something more in his mind.

In late September, Hills was also lining up another Sears purchase — Coldwell Banker, the nation's largest real estate brokerage company — for about $175 million in cash and Sears stock. At the same time, he was talking with Lewis about how to bring Dean Witter into the fold; he hoped that Sears would make both acquisitions at once. The Dean Witter negotiations, however, stumbled over disagreements on price, and the two sides parted company prior to the Sears October 5 announcement of its planned acquisition of Coldwell Banker.

That day, Dean Witter stock began to surge on rumors of a Sears takeover, and by the close of trading on Tuesday it had spurted from $9 a share to $35.25. Andrew Melton, the Dean Witter chairman, was flown to Chicago in the Sears plane on Tuesday to meet again with Telling and revive the merger talks. Two days later, on October 8, Dean Witter's board met in a special six-hour session and unanimously approved the acquisition plan. Sears would pay $50 a share for as much as 45 percent of Dean Witter's stock and would buy the remainder with a like amount of Sears stock.

In discussing the plan that day, Melton pointed to the chain of Wall Street mergers among other financial companies. "It's quite apparent that the alignment of the financial institutions has changed," he said. His merger into Sears, he added, "would make us very competitive."

Indeed, Sears had a customer base of twenty-four million card-holders, which dwarfed Dean Witter's comparatively meager customer list of 650,000. Moreover, seven million of the nine and a half million households that had brokerage accounts were Sears customers.

The Sears deal was the most overt assault on the traditional status of the securities business. Far from the establishment elegance of Wall Street, Sears, based in Chicago, had a distinctly Midwestern image: wholesome, approachable, and unintimidating. It wasn't entrepreneurial, but corporate. "People will buy fertilizer and washing machines from Sears but not stocks and bonds," prophesied one investment banker. Jokesmiths immediately concocted a derisive name for the merged company: Socks 'n Stocks.

Sears immediately answered the cynics with a revolutionary concept for marketing financial services, one that challenged the marketing format Wall Street had followed over the decades. It set up financial counters not far from the large-appliance departments inside a half-dozen of its stores. There, customers could speak with Dean Witter employees about investments, Coldwell Banker people about real estate, or Allstate professionals about insurance.

The novel marketing technique created a rush of business for the Sears financial divisions. More counters appeared in Sears stores around the country. In Cupertino, California, a man walked into a Sears outlet and left more than $3 million in cash and stocks with a Dean Witter broker stationed there. People had come to trust Sears over the years, and this confidence extended to Sears's new brokers. In one store, an elderly woman ranted on at length about her distrust of stockbrokers. When the Dean Witter employee there sheepishly explained that he was a registered broker, she snapped, "No, you're not. You're a Sears employee." Then she opened an account.

Conventional wisdom was again being gainsaid. "There's a new fluidity in the whole distribution mechanism in the United States," said Samuel Hayes, the Jacob Schiff Professor of investment banking at the Harvard Business School. The new owners of Wall Street came from a variety of business disciplines, but they had certain characteristics in common: they were very large, and they saw ways that securities trading and distribution could be linked to other fields.

Other retail firms followed the leader, albeit on a more tentative basis. J. C. Penney entered an agreement with First Nationwide Savings whereby the thrift association set up financial counters in Penney outlets. And the Kroger Company entered a similar agreement with Capital Holding Company.

As the concentration within the financial business continued, there were new pressures on the regional securities firms, which, as a group, had historically provided financing for local enterprises and financial advice to individuals. The pressure came in two ways. With acquisition-minded conglomerates willing to pay top dollar for financial companies, the temptation to sell out was often overwhelming. Moreover, regional securities firms had grave worries that they lacked the capital to compete with the likes of American Express and Sears. Also, independent-minded firms wanted to sell out before the worsening recession affected them. Bruns,

Nordeman, Rea & Company, a New York–based regional firm, in August hired a public relations agency to publicize its status as one of the last privately owned independent securities firms. Later that month, the company was absorbed by Bache, which was itself already held by Prudential. In September, Rauscher Pierce Refsnes, a staunchly independent house based in Dallas, sold itself to Inter-Regional Financial, a smallish Minneapolis-based financial conglomerate, for about $22.7 million. In December 1981, Loewi Financial Company, a securities concern in Milwaukee, agreed to an acquisition by the Kemper Corporation, the Illinois insurance company. Kemper didn't plan to compete with American Express or Merrill Lynch, but neither did the company want to watch itself lose its market share of retail customers who were seeking the convenience of one-stop shopping at the financial conglomerates.

As the year drew to a close, the trend toward amalgamation was intensified by a grave economic slump and a sickening slide in stock prices, which made companies more eager to sell out.

Over the New Year's weekend, Sandy Weill, who for six months had chaired the American Express financial committee as well as Shearson/American Express, headed to Seattle to negotiate a merger. The acquisition target was Foster & Marshall, one of the country's most respected regional houses and the pre-eminent securities house in the Northwest. Weill was eager to show the world, and to assure himself, that Shearson's absorption into American Express had not lessened its appetite for takeovers. He was equally eager to carry out a merger under the banner of American Express, not simply Shearson, whose proposals some firms had spurned in the past.

Foster & Marshall operated fifty-three offices in the Northwest, which meant that Shearson, which had only eight offices there, could quickly expand its presence. The company was controlled by the Foster family; Michael Foster, its chief executive officer and son of the founder, recognized that the firm was at a turning point. Revenue had grown to $72 million in 1981 from $6.5 million in 1972, and Foster & Marshall's workforce had stretched from 240 employees to a thousand in the same period. Now, improved computer systems were needed to process the trading, and even greater capital was required for the firm to compete with the new products that were available at Merrill Lynch and American Express. Merrill Lynch's Cash Management Account alone was attracting six thousand new users each week.

Weill offered ready solutions to these problems. First, Foster & Marshall would dismantle its outmoded operations division and let Shearson process all its business. Second, Shearson's clone of the Merrill Lynch cash management service, to be called the Financial Management Account, would be made available to all the Foster & Marshall customers. Next, the company would be allowed to function as a separate Shearson unit to be known as Foster & Marshall/American Express. The firm readily agreed to a merger.

In February 1982, the Securities and Exchange Commission agreed to new rules for securities underwriting, and these accelerated the merger momentum. Known as Rule 415, the regulations were aimed at simplifying the underwriting process. Under the rule, big corporations would be able to file a single "shelf" registration covering whatever debt or equity offerings they might make for a period of two years. After filing, the corporations would be able to issue debt or equity securities on a moment's notice without any further red tape. The effect was a compression in the time schedule for securities offerings, which suited the skittish character of the markets, where interest rates fluctuated without warning and where companies were encouraged to raise money whenever it seemed affordable. In these short-term underwritings, investment bankers didn't have time to pull together a far-flung syndicate, which would have included smaller regional firms. Instead, a few heavily capitalized firms would join together to buy up all of a securities offering and resell it rapidly to big investing institutions. So the regional houses were shut out of the big underwritings they had once taken part in, and this, in turn, cut into their profits. For some, this was another reason to merge.

In March 1982, American Express bought another regional house, Robinson-Humphrey, a prestigious firm whose home office was in Atlanta. As in the Foster & Marshall deal, the firm was to retain a separate identity, operating as Robinson-Humphrey/American Express. American Express would pay about $77 million in cash and stock for the ninety-year-old securities house.

A week later, Bateman Eichler, a large Los Angeles–based regional firm, put itself on the auction block. Bache negotiated the acquisition of the firm and announced a merger plan, only to have the Kemper Corporation snatch it away with more favorable terms.

The deals continued. In September, the stodgy Mutual Life Insurance Company of Milwaukee, with $12 billion in assets, joined the parade by purchasing Robert W. Baird & Company for $30 million. The same month, Prescott, Ball & Turben, a well-respected Cleveland firm, sold to Kemper for $64 million.

Some regional houses did hang back. For example, Pittsburgh-based Parker/Hunter remained independent and profitable. David Hunter, its chief executive, was openly skeptical about the money giants. "We feel we're riding a good horse," he said. "We have an excellent business, and have since 1894. And nobody's asked us to dance."

Hunter was in the minority. For others, bigness seemed

to be the compelling attraction. With the arrival of the financial conglomerates came the end of the old familial reign on Wall Street. The place was less mysterious and private as it became part of larger, more professionally managed financial marketing concerns. To the old guard, the change was radical and unsettling.

Friends of Billy Salomon said he was both crushed by the news that the firm had been sold and enraged by the callousness of his colleagues, who told him about it two days after everyone in the partnership knew of it. But Billy Salomon's generation was no longer in command.

12

By late 1982, the architects of the new financial business seemed bent on expanding their empires still further. One of the more unusual mergers again involved American Express, which had recognized that someday banking and securities brokerage would be more or less fused. Although U.S. banking statutes in force since 1933 prohibited commercial banks from joining up with investment banks, such a combination was possible in 1982 if the bank was located overseas.

This exception determined the strategy of American Express. The company's headlong expansion into banking services was overseen in late 1982 and early 1983 by Peter Cohen, who had been named president and chief executive officer of Shearson as Sandy Weill took on more responsibilities at

American Express. The merger idea had occurred to Cohen in early 1982 and at the time seemed "a very, very, very long shot." The plan was to acquire Edmond Safra's Trade Development Bank, the highly profitable international bank based in Geneva. Safra, whose family had been in banking since the time of the Ottoman Empire, had met Cohen in 1971 and hired him seven years later to be the chief administrative officer of the Republic National Bank, the U.S. beachhead for Trade Development Bank. Cohen stayed only about a year before returning to Shearson. But he had remained fascinated by Safra, a brilliant and somewhat mysterious man who was considered by some to be the world's richest banker.

In early 1982, when Cohen first thought of the merger, American Express was wrestling with the question of what to do with the American Express International Bank. The unit had performed poorly and was even put on the auction block, but no one came up with a price American Express found acceptable. Sandy Weill advocated holding on to the international bank, believing that someday the barriers between banking and the securities business would be dismantled.

One idea Weill felt should be explored was enlarging the bank through an acquisition, but there were no attractive merger prospects. In October, American Express discouraged overtures from Instituto per le Opere di Religione, generally known as the Vatican Bank, after learning of the bank's possible involvement in the collapse of the scandal-ridden Banco Ambrosiano several months earlier.

On November 7, 1982, Cohen began the pursuit of Edmond Safra. Without telling anyone at Shearson the reason for the trip, he left for Paris, where he had two fourteen-hour discussions with Safra in the banker's apartment. "We talked about the world, about financial services, and about the benefits of the American Express mantle," Cohen said later. On returning to New York, he briefed Weill and Robinson, and urged the latter to use the General Agreement on Tariffs and Trade (GATT) conference in Geneva in late November "as a natural cover for you to meet Safra and get to know him." Robinson agreed, and after meeting Safra in Geneva, flew to Paris with him to discuss a merger of Trade Development into American Express.

Robinson had met Safra earlier and become a strong admirer of his lucrative banking operation. Trade Development's overseas banks had $5.3 billion in total assets and had earned about $60 million in 1982. Like American Express and Shearson, Trade Development Bank shunned strategies that put its own money at risk. It had financial dealings in Brazil but had not made the risky loans to third world countries that had begun to plague other banks. Safra, who went into the banking business at sixteen without a formal education, picked up his conservative banking philosophy from his late father, Jacob Safra.

Independently, a study group at American Express had targeted Trade Development Bank as an institution that the American Express International Bank should emulate by getting into overseas personal banking for the very rich. By the time of Robinson's trip, code words were being used for the project. Trade Development Bank was called Copper, and American Express became Tiger. The entire project was dubbed Mazel Tov, Hebrew words, chosen by Safra, that mean "good luck" or "congratulations."

At a December meeting in New York, Robinson and Safra agreed that a merger made sense. The next meeting, on the New Year's weekend in Paris, was between Sandy Weill and Safra. Still keeping the negotiations secret, Weill told colleagues that he was taking Joan to Paris to cheer her up after the death of her father several weeks earlier. Merger talks with Safra started shortly after the Weills arrived. The two men enjoyed each other's company, so much so that they nearly shattered the secrecy when they decided, at five-fifteen A.M., Paris time, to telephone Cohen at a New Year's Eve party in East Hampton. The telephone was answered by Thomas Strauss, a managing director at Salomon Brothers, who was stunned to hear Safra's name mentioned on the other end. Cohen told him that the call involved the Republic National Bank.

Cohen chose Montreal's Four Seasons Hotel as the site of the final negotiations, because it was relatively close to New York but sufficiently removed to enable him to maintain the secrecy. On Sunday, January 9, Robinson and Safra had each assembled a circle of advisers to negotiate the merger. Cohen was nicknamed "little Kissinger" for his continual shuttling between Safra's camp in Suite 3014 and Robinson's in Suite 2908.

Plans were still incomplete on Monday. Safra then left for Brazil to join his brothers, Joseph and Moïse, at a family gathering in São Paulo. Robinson, meanwhile, flew off to Florida for an executive outing on Malcolm Forbes's yacht.

Back in New York, Cohen worked until four A.M. each night to ready the contract he hoped to sign with Safra when the two groups reconvened the following weekend in Montreal. He also stuck to his normal ten-and-a-half-hour workday to keep other executives from guessing that a merger was in the works.

Robinson cut short the yacht trip to arrange a special meeting of the American Express board for Sunday, January 16, at the Helmsley Palace Hotel in New York. There was also a key management change to ratify: Weill was to become president of American Express, replacing Alva Way, who, recognizing that Weill was actually functioning as the American Express president, had accepted the president's post at Travelers Insurance Companies.

On Saturday, January 15, American Express dispatched its corporate jet to bring Safra from Brazil, where, in addition to visiting his brothers, Safra had gone to visit his father's grave. "Every time I do something, I talk with him about whether it's right or wrong," Safra said later. "I believe he would support me in this."

Sunday night, after the American Express board ratified both the merger plan and the management changes, limousines arrived at the Helmsley Palace to take American Express executives to the Thirty-fourth Street heliport in New York. From there they went to the Westchester airport and boarded two corporate planes for Montreal.

By midnight Sunday, the negotiations at the Four Seasons were back in full swing. Differences over the price and structure of the proposed merger kept the talks going into the morning. At ten A.M. on Monday, Safra's brother Joseph, affectionately known as Jo-Jo, arrived unexpectedly from Brazil, not so much to protect his business interests as simply to be with Edmond at a time of unusual stress. By Monday afternoon, the merger plan seemed in place, and Weill and Robinson returned to New York.

But by the following midnight, Edmond Safra had become distressed at the realization that he was selling part of the family financial empire, and the proceedings halted. Cohen urged Safra to cancel the merger if he didn't feel it was right. The American Express negotiators retired to their suite and began placing bets on whether or when the merger would go through. Close to two A.M., Edmond Safra went into his hotel room with his brother. A few moments later, Jo-Jo Safra left the Trade Development Bank chief alone in the room. And at 2:12 A.M. Safra emerged and said to Cohen, "Let's sign." American Express would buy the bank for about $550 million in cash and securities.

Safra felt the timing of the event was symbolically important. It was now January 18, and, as he explained to Cohen, in Hebrew the word for "18" is the same as the word for "life."

American Express had become the prototype for the new financial services' conglomerate. Its mission was to control assets, not just in the United States, but all over the world. The quickened merger activity spurred by Cohen and Weill since joining the company demonstrated that the Shearson entrepreneurs had indeed breathed new life into American Express. And the livelier American Express convinced Safra of two things: that the financial services' business would eventually be dominated by about twenty-five corporate giants, and that American Express would be one of them.

The international combination came at a time when other Wall Street houses were developing ties around the globe. In 1982, a group of Arab investors bought a 25 percent stake in Smith Barney Harris Upham. And Competrol, a partnership controlled by Saudi Arabian businessmen, had since 1978 built up an expanding stake in Donaldson, Lufkin & Jenrette; by 1982 it stood at just less than 25 percent. Both stock acquisitions were welcome. The foreign investors gave the firms some protection against unwanted predators as well as generous sources of capital. In May 1982, Mercantile House Holdings of London, a leading broker in currencies, agreed to buy Oppenheimer & Company of New York for about $162.5 million. In July, S. G. Warburg & Company, a merchant bank based in London, and Compagnie Financière de Pays Bas, a Paris banking concern, upped their stake in A. G. Becker to a controlling interest after the New York securities firm went through several periods of dropping profits.

In August 1983, Jim Robinson enlisted the aid of Sandy Lewis to help expand the American Express empire further by buying up Investors Diversified Services, a sprawling, Minneapolis-based insurance and mutual fund operation then owned by Allegheny Corporation. Sandy Weill had agreed earlier in the summer to buy IDS and some other Allegheny assets for about $1 billion. However, many within American Express viewed the price as too high, and the firm demanded new terms. The reversal irked Fred Kirby, Allegheny's reclusive and very wealthy chairman, and this made Lewis' task of resurrecting the deal more difficult. Lewis had one advantage, however: a deal his father had swung in the late 1940s had helped create IDS. This bit of history helped get the talks going again, and after several weeks a new merger agreement was announced. American Express would give out fewer of its own shares than stipulated under the first plan and would take on only IDS, not the other Allegheny assets.

Not all of the new combinations were made to last or to continue without disruption. The year 1984, when many securities houses saw slumping profits, brought some significant realignments. Compagnie Financière de Pays Bas, which had by this time purchased S. G. Warburg's stake in A. G. Becker, sold the business to Merrill Lynch. The French banking concern had not been able to reverse Becker's low profitability.

That same year, the relationship between Edmond Safra and American Express turned acrid. Safra's eccentricity and independence, which at first had seemed colorful, became irritating. To avoid possible taxes in the United States, the Trade Development Bank chief stayed outside the country for all of 1983. This meant that business was carried out by telephone or through visits paid by American Express executives to Europe. Safra was difficult to work with, complained one top American Express executive, who rolled his eyes over the banker's habit of carrying wheat germ in his briefcase and his insistence that all his offices in Europe and South America be furnished identically. The secretive Safra never adjusted to working for a big, publicly held corporation. Nor was he pleased by the unexpected slump in American Express stock, of which he was a major holder. While Sandy Weill and Jim Robinson were busy expanding the company's investment and banking activities, Fireman's Fund became badly overextended in the property- and casualty-insurance market and papered over many of its problems through accounting gimmicks. The bottom fell out in late 1983, when the company was forced to take a massive write-off, leading American Express to post a fourth-quarter loss.

In October 1984, Safra announced to the American Express management that he wanted to leave and to cart off the international bank with him. Both sides wanted to avoid a public fracas, so they reached a less radical accord. The settlement allowed Safra to take a portion of the banking empire he had sold to American Express the previous year. And through other parts of the agreement, Safra emerged millions of dollars richer than when he had embarked on the venture with American Express.

Some other merged companies were similarly in flux. In July 1983, Prudential Insurance stripped Harry Jacobs and Virgil Sherrill of their power and brought in as chief executive the forty-four-year-old George Ball, former president of E. F. Hutton Group, Inc. Ball's early efforts to solve Bache's past problems were only modestly successful; both Ball and Prudential conceded that the turnaround would take time. Salomon Brothers continued to post hefty profits after its merger with Phibro, which showed declining returns because of depressed commodities markets. The result was that Salomon became the dominant half of Phibro-Salomon. In August 1984, John Gutfreund of Salomon managed to oust David Tendler, his counterpart at Phibro. That left Gutfreund in control of the entire company.

The money conglomerates were not magically successful, but new mergers continued to be formed. Donaldson, Lufkin & Jenrette, one of the last hold-outs, was bought by the Equitable Life Assurance Society of the United States in 1985. The giant insurer purchased the block of DLJ stock owned by Competrol as part of the deal.

More startling was the acquisition of Lehman Brothers, Kuhn Loeb, Inc., by American Express that same year. Lehman, which had been one of the proudest of privately held investment banks, was thought by many to be the least likely candidate for acquisition by a financial conglomerate. The investment bank was brought down partly by internal strife. In the summer of 1983, the firm fell into disequilibrium. Lewis Glucksman, who had headed the company's trading operations and many of its day-to-day activities, became dissatisfied with his role as co-chief executive officer. The other co-chief executive was Peter Peterson, the former Commerce Secretary, and something of an elder statesman in the financial world. Glucksman, an ambitious and brutally tough infighter, told Peterson, who had promoted him to his position, that he wanted to assume full control of the firm. Peterson, seeking to avoid a rancorous power struggle, decided to give in, explaining to friends that Lehman Brothers was Glucksman's consuming interest, whereas he, Peterson, enjoyed a variety of civic and political involvements.

Once in control, Glucksman began rewarding his friends and disenfranchising those he considered his enemies. Alienated partners, some of whom also felt that the company was undercapitalized for competition with the new financial giants, began exploring the prospect of merging the company out from under Glucksman. Lehman partner Peter Solomon had said in 1983 that Lehman's days were numbered in a world dominated by financial giants like American Express. In early 1984, Solomon pushed talks with Peter Cohen about a takeover. And on April 10, 1984, Lehman Brothers agreed to sell itself to Shearson/American Express. The deal expanded Shearson's investment banking and trading operations and ended Lehman's 134-year history as a private investment bank.

The merger also seemed to settle accounts for Sandy Weill, who had been snubbed in 1978, when Kuhn Loeb rejected the acquisition offer from Shearson in favor of a merger with the more prestigious Lehman Brothers. Now Weill controlled the surviving operations of both firms.

But while Wall Street was being restructured, individual alliances proved ephemeral. Many Lehman partners scattered following the acquisition by Shearson. More important, the partnership between Sandy Weill and Jim Robinson was eroding. Weill, whom many had predicted would quickly ascend to the top spot at the company, was clearly number two to Robinson, who, three years Weill's junior, showed little interest in retirement. And though Weill bore the title of president, his responsibilities shifted frequently and his power base remained vague. Wall Street rumor-mongers, and some widely read financial publications, speculated that the two executives would eventually have some sort of showdown. The two men considered themselves friends and doggedly denied the rumors, but there were tensions, and these were exacerbated by the talk of confrontations.

In December 1983, Weill was called on to rescue the troubled Fireman's Fund Insurance Company. Losses at the San Francisco–based unit had forced American Express to pump in $230 million to bolster reserves. Weill began shuttling to San Francisco every week to control the damage, and others assumed some of his responsibilities back at the home office. Shearson executives, for example, began reporting directly to Robinson, thus diluting Weill's close identification with the Wall Street profit center.

By the fall of 1984, Weill had cut back the insurer's payroll by hundreds and had stemmed the worst of the losses. Ready to resume the pursuit of his goal at American Express, he launched an internal campaign to become, in effect, the chief operating officer of the company, with all the subsidiaries reporting to him. Robinson, under Weill's plan, would continue as the company's chief and as corporate statesman at large, but Weill would be "Mr. Inside."

Weill was rebuffed. Robinson, with the support of the American Express board, favored a decentralized approach, with no one riding herd on the subsidiaries. Under a new alignment of responsibilities, the American Express Travel Services group, the largest single contributor to the firm's revenue, would report to Robinson, as would Shearson and the international bank. Weill would assume responsibilities for the beleaguered Fireman's Fund and for IDS.

Weill was openly unhappy with the arrangement. In May 1985, it occurred to him that the travails of Fireman's Fund might provide a profitable exit. American Express had decided that Fireman's Fund, which mostly offered property and casualty coverage to commercial customers, did not fit well within the corporate scheme of providing financial services to individuals. American Express seemed poised to shed the insurance unit, and Weill approached Robinson with a proposal. "As long as we're talking about the possible disposition of this thing, would you mind if I see whether I can put together something to buy it?" Robinson consented.

Weill then called in investment bankers from Morgan Stanley, takeover attorneys, and several large investors to explore a leveraged buyout of the insurance unit. After several weeks of negotiations, Weill presented American Express with a proposal whereby the company would sell nearly all of its interest in Fireman's Fund to a group of investors he would head up. American Express would retain an interest, so it would stand to profit if Weill succeeded in turning the insurance concern around.

Having made the proposal, Weill left with his wife for a

trip to France to celebrate their thirtieth anniversary. Robinson telephoned him on June 18 to say that the board had rejected the proposal. Weill returned to New York on June 21 and immediately began negotiations with Robinson and various financial and legal advisers. At the outset, he announced that the agenda had changed. "We should talk about my disengaging from the company," he said. On Saturday, he met with the group at the American Express offices; on Sunday, they all met at his home in Greenwich. Late on Monday, the American Express board considered the matter.

On Tuesday morning American Express announced Weill's resignation as president of the company. He was to be replaced by forty-five-year-old Louis Gerstner, Jr. Weill and Robinson met with reporters and displayed the same congeniality they had exhibited when they announced the merger of their two companies four years earlier. The Atlanta patrician and the Brooklyn entrepreneur had been one of corporate America's most interesting odd couples. Each had been a source of fascination for the other, but this was not enough to sustain a lasting partnership. Weill wasn't sure about his next venture; he knew only that he would not accept anything but the lead role.

The business links were not so easily undone, however. Sandy Weill's intuition that the commercial banking and securities businesses would someday be melded together in the United States was partly fired by the Reagan administration's commitment to deregulate American business. It viewed the dismantling of the 1933 financial statutes — which kept the commercial banks out of the core securities business — to be its crowning assault on the New Deal.

So sweeping a change, naturally, wouldn't happen smoothly. Traditional securities firms, which had not aligned with the big corporations during the merger contagion of the early 1980s, wanted to keep the banks out of the underwriting business for fear they would claim too large a share of the profits. These Wall Street firms upped their political contributions to key members of Congress and fought to preserve the 1933 Glass-Steagall Act. Similarly, the insurance business, which was a powerful political force, battled to keep the banks off its turf.

In 1984, the Reagan administration mounted a renewed push to overcome these obstacles and to enact legislation giving the banks more leeway to compete with the likes of American Express and Sears Roebuck. In January, Treasury Secretary Donald Regan and Federal Reserve Board Chairman Paul Volcker boarded a jet headed for Salt Lake City. Regan had joked two days earlier that the critics of the prevailing monetary and fiscal policies might like to see the aircraft go down. The two were scheduled to testify at a hearing in Utah held by Senator Jake Garn, chairman of the Senate Banking Committee. The objective of the Garn hearing was to examine the financial system in light of the revolutionary changes it had undergone. Garn felt that ultimately the laws had to be brought up to date to reflect the new face of the financial business. The focus of debate was the banks, which were both more protected and more regulated than financial conglomerates like American Express. Faced with the new competition from the large money conglomerates, the banks wanted to be unshackled. Regan had once again annoyed Wall Street's old guard, this time by advocating the dismantling of the Glass-Steagall Act and other New Deal financial statutes that crimped the banks. Knowing that he could not push through so radical a change in an election year, he had persuaded Volcker to support a limited liberalization. Banks would be allowed to sell insurance, invest in real estate, offer mutual funds, and underwrite municipal revenue bonds — all new businesses. Garn also supported these new powers for banks. And he swore that if he couldn't get major legislation through Congress in 1984, he would try again the following year.

The Utah session kicked off a series of hearings on the financial business that continued in Washington. At each, Garn would point out that the money business had changed irrevocably during the first years of the 1980s. Banking executives came down hard with the same message. A Citicorp executive vice president, Hans Angermueller, appeared before a House of Representatives group, called the House Wednesday Group, to discuss financial deregulation. Although his bank hadn't previously drawn much sympathy in Washington, the formation of money giants like American Express and Prudential gave him the argument of fairness. "If American Express and Prudential can offer all types of financial services, why can't Citicorp?" Angermueller asked at the House meeting. If one followed Angermueller's reasoning, it would eventually mean the end of the New Deal statutes that had defined the financial system of the post-Depression period by setting banks apart from other financial institutions and restricting their activities.

Many legislators defended the legacy of the 1933 Glass-Steagall Act, which forced the high-flying banks of that era to divest their securities subsidiaries. In those days, the abuses were rampant. Bankers who had securities operations would load up on bad loans, then issue securities in the companies they had lent money to in order to pay themselves back. The public would be left holding the bad paper. Banks were also closing down right and left in the early 1930s, and Congress felt that they would be safer places if they were kept away from the unpredictable and chronically risky stock market.

Since the enactment of Glass-Steagall, concomitant with the creation of the Federal Deposit Insurance Corporation, banks had enjoyed a special position. They were backed by the federal government through the deposit insurance, which gave customers the necessary confidence to allow them to rebuild the ravaged financial system. Along with the insurance came a high degree of regulation: banks could not engage in most forms of commerce and were kept out of other aspects of finance as well. It was considered a reasonable tradeoff. The federal government would stand behind the nation's depository system, but in exchange the banks would have to abide by restrictions. In addition to curbing what business ventures banks could undertake, the McFadden Act kept the banks penned inside state borders. Banks opened up limited operations in more than one state, of course, but none could open full-service branches nationwide.

Outside the legislative arena, banks were pushing up against the boundaries. In December 1982, BankAmerica Corporation, parent of the nation's largest bank, the Bank of America, announced an agreement to buy Charles Schwab & Company, a broker. The Securities Industry Association, bent on keeping the banks out of the business, cried foul and pledged to fight the planned acquisition in the courts. BankAmerica calmly said the deal was perfectly legal under Glass-Steagall because of the nature of Charles Schwab's business. The San Francisco-based firm was the largest discount broker. The discounters were a specialized sliver of the securities business spawned by the 1975 deregulation of brokerage commissions. They didn't underwrite securities or give advice on which stocks to buy, nor did they trade stock with their own capital; they simply took orders over the telephone and executed them. The no-frills brokerage service was offered at a price that could be as much as 80 percent lower than the fees charged by a full-service firm like Merrill Lynch or Shearson. The Glass-Steagall Act specifically prohibited banks from the business of underwriting or distributing securities, but it didn't ban pared-back brokerage operations like Schwab's.

By late 1982, while awaiting approval of the acquisition

by the Federal Reserve Board, the Bank of America began executing trades through Schwab. Then in January of 1983, the Fed bestowed its blessing on the deal, and the acquisition was completed. Other bankers rushed into the discount brokerage business. Security Pacific, based in Los Angeles, began offering customers discount brokerage services directly. Chase Manhattan Bank acquired the Chicago-based Rose & Company. Citicorp set up a joint marketing program with Quick & Reilly, a New York discounter. Chemical Bank offered discount brokerage to customers. Literally hundreds of other banks and thrift companies linked themselves to transaction services as discount brokerage gained popularity.

In 1982, the banks and thrifts waged a successful battle in Washington to be permitted to compete head on with Wall Street's money market funds and cash management services, which had attracted nearly $300 billion from traditional depository accounts. In late 1982, in what amounted to a sweeping deregulation of the interest rates banks paid on deposits, Congress passed the Garn–St Germain Act, which let banks and thrift institutions offer so-called money market deposit accounts. These would, for the first time, provide money market rates on federally insured accounts.

But despite the blurred definitions of financial companies, many in Congress were reluctant to go along with the Reagan administration's efforts to deregulate the banks completely. In 1984, commercial banks were failing at a post-Depression record, which made Congress hesitant to give banks new business opportunities. In addition, during the summer of 1984, the Continental Illinois Bank experienced an international run on its deposits and was saved only through a $4.5 billion government rescue. For many members of Congress, the Continental crisis, which could have turned into a broader banking panic, was sufficient grounds for continuing restrictions of banks' activities.

The bank deregulation plan, however, wouldn't go away. The financial system was essentially different. Sears and American Express could diversify in ways the commercial banks could not do under the law, and the bankers argued that this was unfair. Others who tried to keep the different financial businesses separate, as they had been for most of the fifty years following the 1933 banking crisis, had difficulty making their arguments hold up. During Senate hearings, an insurance man argued strenuously that banks should not be allowed to expand into the insurance trade. Senator Garn rebutted by pointing to the mergers of 1981. "Should Prudential get rid of Bache? Should American Express get rid of Shearson? If everybody had wanted to remain in their own business, we wouldn't be here. If securities firms wanted to be securities firms, and if banks wanted to be banks, we could do something else." As a banker attending the hearing observed afterward, the genie was out of the bottle, and the U.S. financial system would never be the same again.

Timothy Carrington, author of
THE YEAR THEY SOLD WALL STREET
Published by Houghton Mifflin Company,
December 12, 1985. Photo by Jerry Bauer

Index

About the Author

A graduate of the University of Virginia, Tim Carrington is a reporter for the *Wall Street Journal*. From 1980 to 1984 he covered the securities business for the New York bureau, and at present he is the Pentagon correspondent in Washington, where he lives with his wife and two sons. He has also served as Managing Editor for *Securities Week*. *The Year They Sold Wall Street* is his first book.